Contents

Let's Go Camping!

My family likes to camp in the mountains every summer. We find a good spot near the lake to pitch our tent. That makes it easy to swim whenever we like. My brother and I look for firewood while Mom and Dad set up camp. Then we light a big fire. My family tells stories around the fire until we can't stay awake any longer. The next day, we pack a lunch. We get water to drink. We have a new boat this year. It's bigger than our old boat. We can't wait to put our boat in the lake. We'll sail over to Pine Island to go exploring. I wonder what we'll find?

Find It! Read the spelling words.
Check off the words you can find in the story.

☐ pitch	☐ drink	☐ swim	☐ while	☐ light
☐ which	☐ find	☐ fire	☐ tent	☐ camp

How many spelling words did you find? ______

Skills:

Spelling Words with Long and Short **i**

Spelling Theme Vocabulary

Visual Memory

Spelling Practice

Read and Spell	Copy and Spell	Spell It Again!
1. pitch		
2. drink		
3. swim		
4. which		
5. light		
6. while		
7. find		
8. fire		
9. tent		
10. camp		

Find the Words

Write the missing spelling words to complete the sentences.

1. Let's ____________ our ____________ near the lake.

which | tent | pitch

2. I can ____________ ____________ you fish for dinner.

while | swim | tent

3. We will ____________ the ____________ to toast marshmallows.

pitch | fire | light

4. Did you ____________ a good place to ____________?

drink | find | camp

5. That ____________, ____________ is sweet, tastes good!

which | tent | drink

Skills:

Words with Long and Short **i**

Spelling Theme Vocabulary

Using Context Clues to Find Missing Words

Skills:

Visual Memory and Discrimination

Scrambled Words

Unscramble each word and write it on the line. Then match it to the correct spelling.

1. difn	find	tent
2. elwhi	____________	pitch
3. pihct	____________	light
4. ntet	____________	which
5. gthli	____________	drink
6. frei	____________	find
7. cpma	____________	swim
8. dirkn	____________	fire
9. chwih	____________	camp
10. wims	____________	while

Match the Meanings

Skills:

Matching Words with Their Meanings

Write the letter of the definition next to the spelling word.

_______ 1. find	a. during the time that something else is happening
_______ 2. while	b. a portable shelter held up by poles
_______ 3. pitch	c. to come across something
_______ 4. tent	d. to move through the water using the arms and legs
_______ 5. light	e. to put up a tent
_______ 6. fire	f. to swallow liquid
_______ 7. camp	g. flames, heat, and light produced by burning
_______ 8. drink	h. to live or stay outdoors
_______ 9. swim	i. to start something burning
_______ 10. which	j. a particular one

Skills:

Identifying Proper and Common Nouns

Capitalizing Proper Nouns

Naming Things

Nouns name a person, place, or thing.

- Common nouns name any person, place, or thing. They do not begin with a capital letter.

sister	doctor	deer

- **Proper nouns** name a specific person, place, or thing. They begin with a capital letter.

Idaho	Dr. Drake	Lake Tahoe

Cross out any letter that should be a capital letter. Then write the capital letter above it.

1. mount whitney
2. girl
3. forest ranger
4. mr. thompson
5. camp shasta
6. crystal lake
7. forest
8. brother
9. justin
10. pine tree
11. pine island
12. blue jay
13. montana
14. waterfall

Spellamadoodle

Skills:

Writing Spelling Words

Write each spelling word on the outline of the drawing. You may use the words more than once. For fun, decorate the drawing.

light	tent	fire	pitch	swim
find	which	camp	while	drink

Skills:

Writing a List

What Should I Bring?

Pretend you are going camping with your family. There is a lake, hiking trails, and a lot of different animals. What will you bring? Make a list below.

My Camping Checklist

sleeping bag

swimsuit

Dear Friend . . .

Skills:

Writing a Postcard

You are on a camping trip with your family. Write a postcard to a friend. Tell your friend all about the fun things you are doing! Use as many spelling words as you can.

light	tent	fire	pitch	swim
find	which	camp	while	drink

To:

Check Your Writing

- ○ I used a capital letter for each name.
- ○ I checked my spelling.

TEST YOUR SKILLS

Let's Go Camping!

Find the correct answer. Fill in the circle.

1. Which sentence has the correct capital letters?
   - ◯ Ranger Moore showed us Rabbit Trail.
   - ◯ My brother jake caught fish in Mirror lake.
   - ◯ Camp Canoe is open all Summer long.

2. Which sentence has the correct capital letters?
   - ◯ My Family hiked on Mt. red rock.
   - ◯ We visited Red Rock Museum today.
   - ◯ We saw many Deer at Breezy meadow.

3. Which word is spelled correctly?
   - ◯ light
   - ◯ lite
   - ◯ lighte

4. Which word means "to discover or come across something"?
   - ◯ pitch
   - ◯ find
   - ◯ which

My Spelling Test

Ask someone to test you on the spelling words.

1. ____________________
2. ____________________
3. ____________________
4. ____________________
5. ____________________
6. ____________________
7. ____________________
8. ____________________
9. ____________________
10. ____________________

5. Write the sentence correctly.

dad can let us swum wille he lites the fire

____

____

At the Library

The new library opened this weekend, and Dad took us to see it. There were many new things to see inside. I believe there are thousands of new books. The children's room is amazing! One bench has two friendly bears sitting on it. You can sit between the bears and read a book. There are several computers, and someone is always there to help you. We took a tour and learned about the number system that keeps the books in order. It was easy for me to find my favorite author. We left after the tour, but Dad said we could go again next week.

Find It! Read the spelling words.
Check off the words you can find in the story.

☐ next	☐ left	☐ help	☐ please	☐ believe
☐ many	☐ between	☐ order	☐ author	☐ title

How many spelling words did you find? ______

Skills:

Spelling Words with Long and Short **e**

Spelling Theme Vocabulary

Visual Memory

Spelling Practice

Read and Spell	Copy and Spell	Spell It Again!
1. next	__________	__________
2. left	__________	__________
3. help	__________	__________
4. please	__________	__________
5. believe	__________	__________
6. many	__________	__________
7. between	__________	__________
8. order	__________	__________
9. author	__________	__________
10. title	__________	__________

Word Study

Read the words. Write them in the correct column. One word will be in both columns.

help	please	between	next
believe	left	many	

Sound of e as in eat	Sound of e as in bed
______________	______________
______________	______________
______________	______________
______________	______________

Circle the correctly spelled word in each row.

1.	oredr	order	ordur
2.	menny	manny	many
3.	author	ather	awther
4.	pleese	please	pleez
5.	title	tiet	tittel

Skills:

Spelling Words with Long and Short **e**

Spelling Theme Vocabulary

Auditory Discrimination

Skills:

Spelling Words with Long and Short **e**

Spelling Theme Vocabulary

Spelling Words

Fill in the missing letters to make spelling words.

next	left	help	please	believe
many	between	order	author	title

1. pl ____ ____ se
2. l ____ ft
3. betw ____ ____ n
4. m ____ ny
5. n ____ xt
6. t ____ ____ le
7. ____ ____ der
8. h ____ lp
9. bel ____ ____ ve
10. ____ ____ thor

Picking Pronouns

Skills:

Replacing Nouns with Pronouns

A **pronoun** is a word that takes the place of one or more nouns.

Jenna works at the library. She works at the library.

Use the pronouns below to replace the underlined words. Write the pronouns on the line. You will use some pronouns more than once.

he **she** **you** **it** **they** **them**

1. I believe Tanya checked out that book already. ________
2. You can find books on many shelves. ________
3. Chad likes books about dinosaurs. ________
4. My mom read aloud books to the children. ________
5. Children can sit between the bears to read. ________
6. Please help me look up titles on the computer. ________
7. These books are in a certain order. ________
8. Dad left us in the children's room to read. ________

Which Word?

Write the missing words on the lines.

1. Margie chose her book ______________.

believe next help

2. Trey is the ______________ of this book.

many please author

3. Can you read the ______________ of this book?

title between many

4. Dad will ______________ us at the library.

help author title

5. Jack sat ______________ both bears on the bench.

please next between

6. I found so ______________ books at the new library.

many please author

7. We ______________ after the tour.

order left please

8. I learned what ______________ the books are in.

please left order

Spellamadoodle

Write each spelling word on the outline of the drawing. You may use the words more than once. For fun, decorate the drawing.

next	left	help	please	believe
many	between	order	author	title

Skills:

Writing Spelling Words

Skills:

Writing a List

Writing Descriptions

My Favorite Books

Do you visit the library often? What are some of the books you've read? List the titles of your three favorite books. Then write what each book was about.

My 3 Favorites

1 Title

2 Title

3 Title

Library Visit

Skills:

Writing a Personal Narrative

Have you been to the library? What do you like to do there? How do you find the books you want? Describe a trip to the library. Use as many spelling words as you can.

next	left	help	please	believe
many	between	order	author	title

Check Your Writing

- ❍ I used a capital letter to begin each sentence.
- ❍ I used a period to end each sentence.
- ❍ I checked my spelling.

TEST YOUR SKILLS

At the Library

Find the correct answer. Fill in the circle.

1. Which pronoun would you use to replace the word **Maria**?
   - ❍ the
   - ❍ she
   - ❍ they

2. Which pronoun would you use to replace **the computer**?
   - ❍ she
   - ❍ they
   - ❍ it

3. Which word is spelled correctly?
   - ❍ many
   - ❍ meny
   - ❍ manny

4. Which word means "the writer of a book, play, or poem"?
   - ❍ title
   - ❍ author
   - ❍ order

My Spelling Test

Ask someone to test you on the spelling words.

1. ____________________
2. ____________________
3. ____________________
4. ____________________
5. ____________________
6. ____________________
7. ____________________
8. ____________________
9. ____________________
10. ____________________

5. Write the sentence correctly.

we belleves this titel is nekst for our author

____

____

Sports, Sports, Sports

Everyone in my family likes to play sports. My mom is the coach of my softball team. We are called the Eastside Earthquakes. We won our city championship last season.

My big brother has a skateboard. He takes it to Irvine Skateboard Park to practice. Sometimes my friends and I go to watch.

When we finish our homework, my sister and I like to play basketball outside. My dad put up a hoop in the driveway. Sometimes he plays, too. Each time you throw the ball into the basket, you get a point. The first one to get twenty-one points wins.

Almost everybody I know is on some kind of sports team. Sports are not only fun, but also great exercise. What's your favorite sport?

Find It! Read the spelling words.
Check off the words you can find in the story.

- [ ] point
- [ ] coach
- [ ] everybody
- [ ] everyone
- [ ] basketball
- [ ] tie
- [ ] outside
- [ ] skateboard
- [ ] earthquake
- [ ] homework

How many spelling words did you find? ______

Skills:

Compound Words

Spelling Theme Vocabulary

Visual Memory

Spelling Practice

Read and Spell	Copy and Spell	Spell It Again!
1. point	______	______
2. coach	______	______
3. tie	______	______
4. everybody	______	______
5. everyone	______	______
6. outside	______	______
7. basketball	______	______
8. skateboard	______	______
9. earthquake	______	______
10. homework	______	______

Two Words Make One

Draw a line between two words to make compound spelling words.

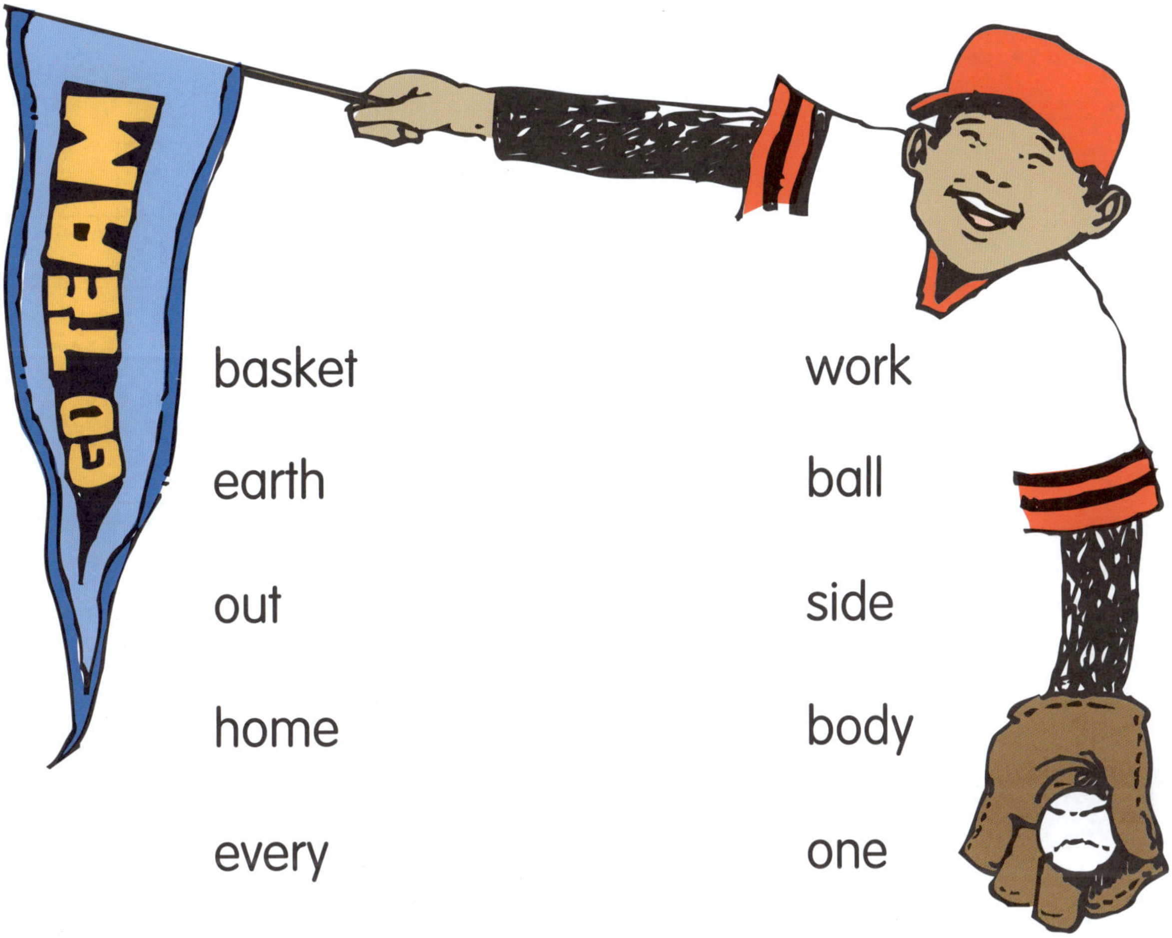

basket	work
earth	ball
out	side
home	body
every	one
skate	quake
every	board

Skills:

Compound Words

Spelling Theme Vocabulary

Visual Memory

Mini-Crosswords

Complete the crossword puzzles using nine of the spelling words.

point	coach	tie	everybody	everyone
outside	basketball	skateboard	earthquake	homework

1.

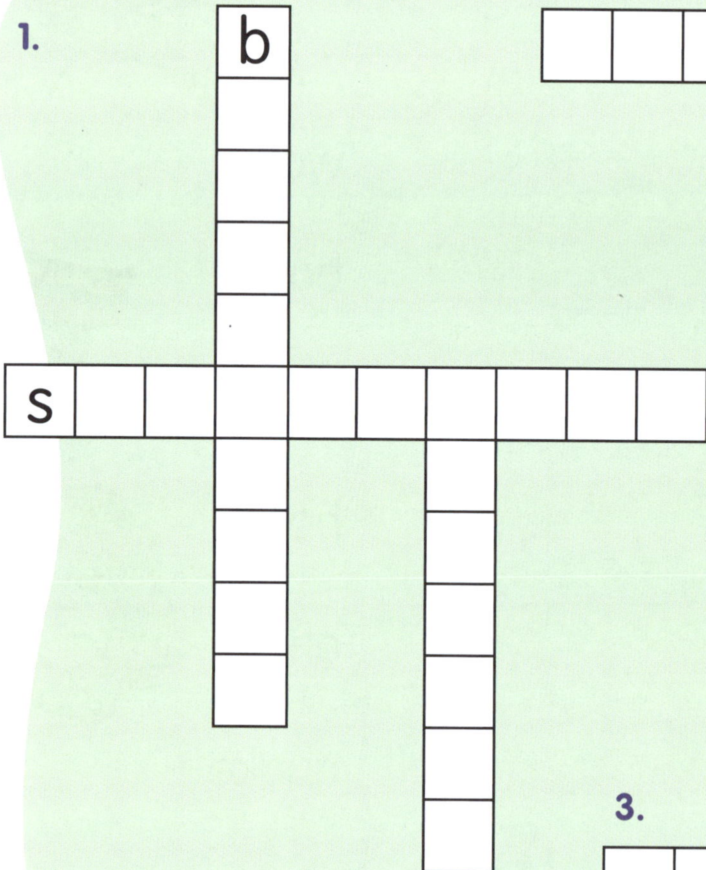

2.

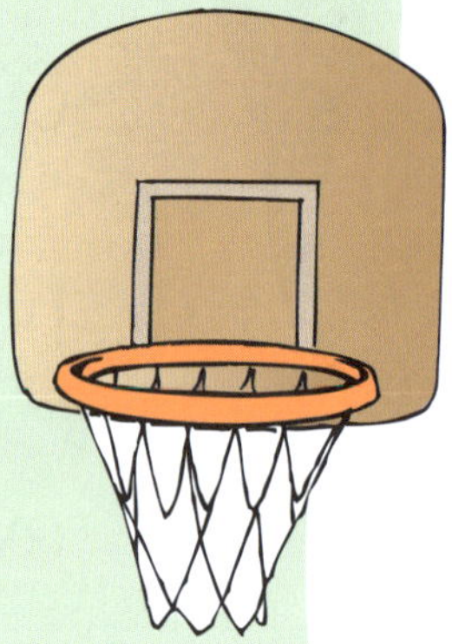

3.

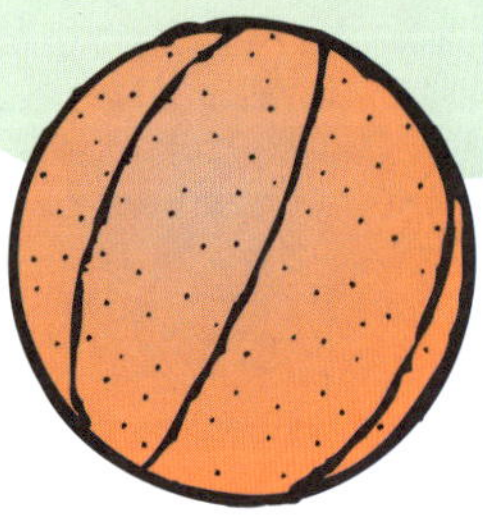

Which Part Is It?

Skills:

Identifying Subjects and Predicates

Every complete sentence has two parts.

- A subject is the part that names the main person, place, or thing.
- A predicate is the part that tells what the subject is or does.

My mom bought me a basketball.

Circle the subject and underline the predicate.

1. My brother rides his skateboard at the park.
2. Our softball team won the championship.
3. Each player had several turns at bat.
4. Staci hit a home run in the sixth inning.
5. My whole family plays sports together.

Skills:

Matching Words with Their Meanings

Make a Match

Write the letter of the definition next to the word.

_____ 1. point

_____ 2. outside

_____ 3. coach

_____ 4. basketball

_____ 5. tie

_____ 6. skateboard

_____ 7. everyone/everybody

_____ 8. earthquake

_____ 9. homework

a. one who trains a sports team

b. sudden violent shaking of the earth

c. board with wheels that you stand on and ride

d. each and every person

e. unit for scoring in a game

f. schoolwork done at home

g. game played by 2 teams of 5 players each

h. when 2 teams have the same score

i. out of a building, or in the open air

Spellamadoodle

Skills:

Writing
Spelling
Words

Write each spelling word on the outline of the drawing. You may use the words more than once. For fun, decorate the drawing.

point	coach	tie	everybody	everyone
outside	basketball	skateboard	earthquake	homework

Skills:

Writing an Opinion Paper

My Favorite Sport

What is your favorite sport? Do you like team sports like baseball? Or do you like to play on your own, like tennis? Write about your favorite sport below. Describe what you like about it.

The Great Game

Skills:

Writing a Sports Story

Using your favorite sport, write about a great game. Write about what happened. Who were the teams? Who won? Tell about a game you actually saw or played, or make up a game. Use as many spelling words as you can.

point	coach	tie	everybody	everyone
outside	basketball	skateboard	earthquake	homework

Check Your Writing

- ◯ I used complete sentences.
- ◯ I used correct spelling.
- ◯ I used correct capitalization and punctuation.

TEST YOUR SKILLS

Sports, Sports, Sports

Find the correct answer. Fill in the circle.

1. In which sentence does the line separate the subject and the predicate?
   - ❍ Torey's coach / took the team to the state finals.
   - ❍ Torey's / coach took the team to the state finals.
   - ❍ Torey's coach took / the team to the state finals.

2. In which sentence does the line separate the subject and predicate?
   - ❍ Michael played / soccer last year.
   - ❍ Michael / played soccer last year.
   - ❍ Michael player soccer / last year.

3. Which word is spelled correctly?
   - ❍ skatboarde
   - ❍ skateborde
   - ❍ skateboard

4. Which word means "a situation when two teams have the same score"?
   - ❍ tie
   - ❍ point
   - ❍ river

My Spelling Test

Ask someone to test you on the spelling words.

1. ______________________
2. ______________________
3. ______________________
4. ______________________
5. ______________________
6. ______________________
7. ______________________
8. ______________________
9. ______________________
10. ______________________

5. Write the sentence correctly.

our coche told evrybody to play bassketball outside

____

____

Family Rap

People who love you,
People who share,
They're the ones
Who'll always care.
A family.

People together,
People who say,
"We're proud of you
In every way."
A family.

People who help you,
People who make
A home that's happy.
It's no mistake.
A family.

People who know you,
People who see
All that you are,
And all you can be.
A family.

Find It!

Read the spelling words.
Check off the words you can find in the story.

- [ ] I'm
- [ ] it's
- [ ] they're
- [ ] we're
- [ ] o'clock
- [ ] let's
- [ ] together
- [ ] home
- [ ] family
- [ ] that's

How many spelling words did you find? ______

Skills:

Contractions

Spelling Theme Vocabulary

Visual Memory

Spelling Practice

Read and Spell	Copy and Spell	Spell It Again!
1. I'm		
2. it's		
3. they're		
4. we're		
5. that's		
6. o'clock		
7. let's		
8. together		
9. home		
10. family		

Match and Spell

Skills:

Contractions

Spelling Theme Vocabulary

Visual Memory

Draw a line between the two words that make each contraction. Write the word on the line.

I'm they're we're let's it's that's

let	is	______________
they	are	______________
that	is	______________
I	are	______________
we	us	______________
it	am	______________

Skills:

Contractions

Spelling Theme Vocabulary

Visual Memory

Spell It

Circle the correctly spelled word in each row.

1.	were’	we’re	wee’re
2.	hume	homme	home
3.	toogeter	together	tugethr
4.	let’s	lett’s	lets’
5.	family	fammile	famully
6.	thayre	they’er	they’re
7.	oh’clock	o’clock	o’clocke
8.	tha’ts	thats’	that’s
9.	I’m	I’am	I’me
10.	i’ts	its’	it’s

Contraction Action

Skills:

Using Apostrophes to Make Contractions

Use an apostrophe (') when making a contraction. The apostrophe takes the place of the missing letter or letters.

let us let's I am I'm

Cross out the letter or letters in each set of words to make a contraction. Replace the letter or letters with an apostrophe. Write the contraction on the line. The first one has been done for you.

1. we	will	we'll
2. have	not	________
3. I	will	________
4. they	are	________
5. he	is	________
6. it	is	________
7. can	not	________
8. did	not	________

Skills:

Visual Memory

Contractions

Circle It!

Circle the correct spelling.

1. **Ime/I'm** going to my soccer game.
2. My **famile/family** is coming to watch.
3. The game starts at four **o'clock/oklock**.
4. **It's/Its** going to be a good game.
5. **Weer'e/We're** going out for pizza afterward.
6. They know **that's/that'ts** my favorite food.

Spellamadoodle

Write each spelling word on the outline of the drawing. You may use the words more than once. For fun, decorate the drawing.

I'm	it's	they're	we're	o'clock
let's	together	home	family	that's

Skills:

Writing Spelling Words

Skills:

Writing a Poem

Families Care

Write a poem using the letters in the word **family**. Think of all the ways your family cares for you. Then write something that starts with each letter in the word. Your poem does not have to rhyme.

Examples:

Feeds and clothes me

Always there for me

F ______________________

A ______________________

M ______________________

I ______________________

L ______________________

Y ______________________

My Family Is Special

What makes your family special? Do you share a special tradition, event, talent, or relative? Write about your family below. Use as many spelling words as you can.

I'm	it's	they're	we're	o'clock
let's	together	home	family	that's

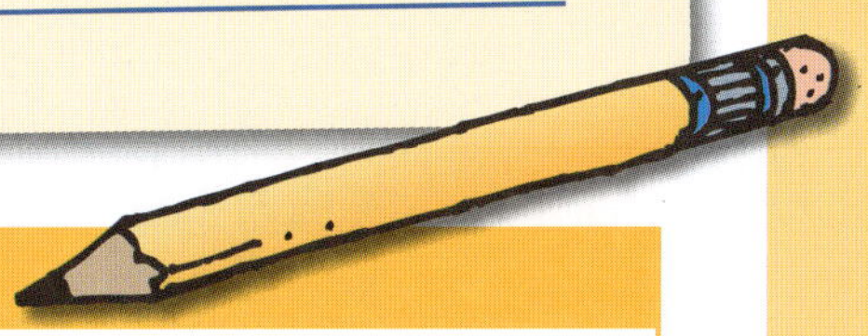

✓ Check Your Writing

- ◯ I used a capital letter for each name.
- ◯ I checked my spelling.

Skills:

Writing a Personal Narrative

TEST YOUR SKILLS

Family Rap

Find the correct answer. Fill in the circle.

1. Which contraction is made up of the two underlined words?

   Jenny <u>does not</u> want to leave her family.

   - ◯ don't
   - ◯ doesn't
   - ◯ didn't

2. Which contraction is made up of the two underlined words?

   Mando <u>is not</u> ready for his test.

   - ◯ won't
   - ◯ it's
   - ◯ isn't

3. Which word is spelled correctly?
   - ◯ familly
   - ◯ family
   - ◯ famly

4. Which word means "a place where you live or belong"?
   - ◯ home
   - ◯ o'clock
   - ◯ it's

My Spelling Test

Ask someone to test you on the spelling words.

1. ______________________
2. ______________________
3. ______________________
4. ______________________
5. ______________________
6. ______________________
7. ______________________
8. ______________________
9. ______________________
10. ______________________

5. Write the sentence correctly.

   letts get tugethr when theyre finished

   ____

   ____

Mystery Map

I found an old map on the playground. The map shows a river. In the middle of the river are three islands. One of them looks different because it has a huge X on it. This is a mystery! I think it shows where a forgotten treasure is hidden. Maybe it's gold coins or jewels. Do you want to help me look for it? We need to find it before it disappears. Meet me at the tunnel near the playground. Bring your backpack with the zipper and a compass. We might have to carry something back. Get ready to solve the mystery!

Find It! Read the spelling words.
Check off the words you can find in the story.

- [ ] letter
- [ ] different
- [ ] pattern
- [ ] middle
- [ ] zipper
- [ ] carry
- [ ] Mississippi
- [ ] compass
- [ ] backpack
- [ ] river

How many spelling words did you find? ______

Skills:

Spelling Words with Double Consonants

Spelling Theme Vocabulary

Visual Memory

Spelling Practice

Read and Spell	Copy and Spell	Spell It Again!
1. letter	__________	__________
2. different	__________	__________
3. pattern	__________	__________
4. middle	__________	__________
5. Mississippi	__________	__________
6. zipper	__________	__________
7. carry	__________	__________
8. compass	__________	__________
9. backpack	__________	__________
10. river	__________	__________

Word Study

Fill in the missing double letters to make spelling words.

le ____ ____ er   pa ____ ____ ern

compa ____ ____   ca ____ ____ y

di ____ ____erent   zi ____ ____ er

mi ____ ____ le   Mi ____ ____ issi ____ ____ i

Circle each spelling word.

compassrivermiddlelettercarryzipperbackpack

differentpatterncarrybackpackmiddleMississippi

letterMississippizipperrivercompasspatterndifferent

Skills:

Spelling Words with Double Consonants

Spelling Theme Vocabulary

Visual Memory and Discrimination

Skills:

Spelling Words with Double Consonants

Spelling Theme Vocabulary

Matching Words with Their Meanings

Crossword Challenge

Complete the crossword puzzle using words from the spelling list. You will not use one word.

letter	different	pattern	middle	Mississippi
zipper	carry	compass	backpack	river

Across

2. halfway between two things
5. a repeating arrangement of colors, shapes, and figures
7. to hold something and take it somewhere
8. a message that you write to someone
9. an instrument for finding directions

Down

1. a fastener for clothes or other objects
3. not the same
4. a large bag you carry on your back
6. a large natural stream of fresh water

Word Search

Skills:

Visual Sequencing

Recognizing Spelling Words

Find and circle each spelling word. Words can go across, down, or diagonally.

letter	different	pattern	middle	Mississippi
zipper	carry	compass	backpack	river

K	T	S	S	A	P	M	O	C	I	A	N
C	A	N	A	I	L	Y	O	U	Z	U	R
A	K	I	E	A	R	E	O	R	I	Z	E
P	E	A	R	R	O	I	T	O	P	I	T
K	R	E	A	K	E	I	V	T	P	A	T
C	L	C	A	K	E	F	L	E	E	R	A
A	S	K	F	O	R	I	F	O	R	R	P
B	M	I	S	S	I	S	S	I	P	P	I
S	O	M	E	W	H	M	I	D	D	L	E

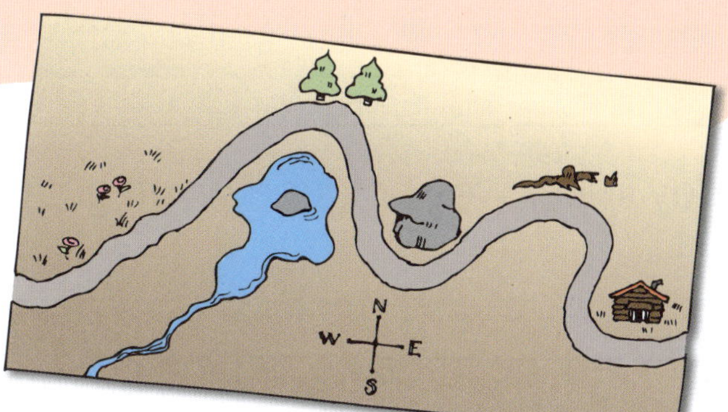

Skills:

Using Capital Letters

Capital Letters

Use a capital letter to begin:

- a sentence

We found a map.

- days of the week, months of the year, and holidays

Tuesday October Halloween

- names of specific persons, places, or things

Jason Alabama Red Rock

Circle each word that needs a capital letter. Write the capitalized words on the lines.

1. i read a mystery about two kids named wyatt and dylan.

____

2. they were in hawaii looking for buried treasure.

____

3. all summer, their friend jenna helped with the search.

____

4. on a tuesday, dylan finally found a big clue.

____

5. this clue led them up the side of mount jade.

____

6. this day in july was hot, and wyatt got tired.

____

7. jenna found the treasure behind crystal falls.

____

Spellamadoodle

Skills:

Writing Spelling Words

Write each spelling word on the outline of the drawing. You may use the words more than once. For fun, decorate the drawing.

letter	different	pattern	middle	Mississippi
zipper	carry	compass	backpack	river

Skills:

Writing a Description

The Perfect Treasure

If you found a mystery map, where would you like it to lead? What treasure would you like to find? Describe your perfect treasure below.

Check Your Writing

- ❍ I used a capital letter to begin each sentence.
- ❍ I used a capital letter for each proper noun.
- ❍ I checked my spelling.

My Own Mystery Map

Think of a good place at school or in your neighborhood to hide buried treasure. Then write directions for how to find it! Draw a map to go with your directions below.

First, ______________________________ .

Second, ______________________________ .

Third, ______________________________ .

Then, ______________________________ .

Next, ______________________________ .

Last, ______________________________ .

Skills:

Writing Directions

Drawing a Map

TEST YOUR SKILLS

Mystery Map

Find the correct answer. Fill in the circle.

1. Which sentence has correct capital letters?
   - ◯ fourth of july is my favorite Summer holiday.
   - ◯ On saturday, we'll try to find the treasure.
   - ◯ Ms. Owens is coming to visit in March.

2. Which noun should be capitalized?
   - ◯ brother
   - ◯ museum
   - ◯ noah

3. Which word is spelled correctly?
   - ◯ different
   - ◯ diffrent
   - ◯ diffrete

4. Which word means "halfway between two things"?
   - ◯ pattern
   - ◯ middle
   - ◯ carry

My Spelling Test

Ask someone to test you on the spelling words.

1. ____________________
2. ____________________
3. ____________________
4. ____________________
5. ____________________
6. ____________________
7. ____________________
8. ____________________
9. ____________________
10. ____________________

5. Write the sentence correctly.

   get your cumpass and your bakpak with the zippere

   ____

   ____

Money Matters

My grandpa is teaching me an important lesson—how to save my money. He has given me fifty dollars for my birthday every year. He takes me to the bank where I have an account. The bank teller puts the money in my account, and she writes the amount in my bankbook. Do you know what the bank does? It pays me for using my money!

Grandpa showed me how to save some money in a change jar, too. I put in quarters, dimes, nickels, and pennies. When the jar is full, I count the money. Then I put it into two piles. I keep one pile to spend, and I take the other to the bank. I like to read my bankbook. I can see my savings grow.

Find It! Read the spelling words.
Check off the words you can find in the story.

- [ ] again
- [ ] given
- [ ] other
- [ ] does
- [ ] some
- [ ] money
- [ ] change
- [ ] read
- [ ] bank
- [ ] save

How many spelling words did you find? ______

Skills:

Spelling Words with the **Schwa** Sound

Spelling Theme Vocabulary

Visual Memory

Spelling Practice

Read and Spell	Copy and Spell	Spell It Again!
1. again	______	______
2. given	______	______
3. other	______	______
4. does	______	______
5. some	______	______
6. money	______	______
7. change	______	______
8. read	______	______
9. bank	______	______
10. save	______	______

Word Study

Skills:

Spelling Words with the **Schwa** Sound

Spelling Theme Vocabulary

Visual Memory

Auditory Discrimination

Circle the letter or letters in each word that make the sound of o in ton.

again does money
other some

Unscramble the letters to make spelling words. Write them on the lines.

1. igana ________________
2. eghacn ________________
3. vgein ________________
4. erhot ________________
5. nbka ________________
6. vesa ________________
7. eosd ________________
8. yeonm ________________
9. edra ________________
10. moes ________________

Skills:

Spelling Words with the **Schwa** Sound

Spelling Theme Vocabulary

Visual Memory

Spelling in Context

Write It Right

Circle the misspelled words. Write them correctly on the lines.

1. Let's take our munny to the banck.

   ____________ ____________

2. Mom has givvan me sum coins.

   ____________ ____________

3. Dous the teller help you make chanje?

   ____________ ____________

4. I can reade what I sav in my bankbook.

   ____________ ____________

5. My uther piggy bank is full agane.

   ____________ ____________

Kinds of Sentences

Skills:

Identifying Different Kinds of Sentences

Using Correct Ending Punctuation

There are four kinds of sentences. Each kind uses specific ending punctuation.

- A statement tells something. It ends with a period. (.)
- A question asks something. It ends with a question mark. (?)
- A command tells someone to do something. It ends with a period. (.)
- An exclamation shows strong feeling. It ends with an exclamation mark. (!)

Add the correct ending punctuation. Then write whether each sentence is a **statement**, **question**, **command**, or **exclamation**.

1. Did you count all your money _____ _______________
2. Put your money in the bank _____ _______________
3. Wow, look at all that money _____ _______________
4. The bank is behind the library _____ _______________
5. Who is the bank teller today _____ _______________
6. My house is on fire _____ _______________
7. Did you save enough for a coat _____ _______________
8. Count this change _____ _______________

Skills:

Matching Words with Their Meanings

Make a Match

Draw a line from each spelling word to its meaning.

again	different, not the same
given	performing an action
other	to keep money to use in the future
does	one more time
some	coins, not bills
money	coins and bills people use to buy things
change	an amount that is not named
read	a place where people keep their money
bank	to have handed something to another person
save	to look at written words and understand what they mean

Spellamadoodle

Skills:

Writing
Spelling
Words

Write each spelling word on the outline of the drawing. You may use the words more than once. For fun, decorate the drawing.

again	given	other	does	some
money	change	read	bank	save

Skills:

Writing a List

Lots of Money

You just won first place in a contest! You won $10,000! What are you going to do with the money? Buy presents? Save it in the bank? Go on a trip? List ten things you would do with the money.

1. ____________________
2. ____________________
3. ____________________
4. ____________________
5. ____________________
6. ____________________
7. ____________________
8. ____________________
9. ____________________
10. ____________________

Lost and Found

Skills:

Writing a Creative Story

You've just found a wallet at the park. It's stuffed full of money! What will you do with it? Write your story below. Use as many spelling words as you can.

again	given	other	does	some
money	change	read	bank	save

Check Your Writing

- ◯ I used a capital letter to begin each sentence.
- ◯ I used correct punctuation at the end of each sentence.
- ◯ I checked my spelling.

TEST YOUR SKILLS

Money Matters

Find the correct answer. Fill in the circle.

1. What kind of sentence is this?

   Did you save your money in that jar?

   - ❍ statement
   - ❍ question
   - ❍ command
   - ❍ exclamation

2. What kind of sentence is this?

   Come with me to the bank.

   - ❍ statement
   - ❍ question
   - ❍ command
   - ❍ exclamation

3. Which word is spelled correctly?

   - ❍ chanje
   - ❍ chainge
   - ❍ change

4. Which word means "different, not the same as mentioned"?

   - ❍ other
   - ❍ some
   - ❍ again

My Spelling Test

Ask someone to test you on the spelling words.

1. ______________________
2. ______________________
3. ______________________
4. ______________________
5. ______________________
6. ______________________
7. ______________________
8. ______________________
9. ______________________
10. ______________________

5. Write the sentence correctly.

   they have given me monny to savve in the banck

   ____

   ____

Washington, D.C.

There are many places to see in Washington, D.C. This great city is the capital of the United States. We went with a group of people to see the White House. That is the house where the president lives. The White House was built in 1800! The address is 1600 Pennsylvania Avenue. Around town, there are many parks and museums to visit. We saw a tall white tower named after George Washington. It is called the Washington Monument. We also found a place where you can see airplanes and rockets. It is called the Smithsonian Institute. There are so many things to see in this city. I couldn't see everything. I hope that someday I can visit Washington, D.C., again.

Find It! Read the spelling words.
Check off the words you can find in the story.

☐ town	☐ found	☐ about	☐ house	☐ group
☐ country	☐ around	☐ bridge	☐ tower	☐ park

How many spelling words did you find? ______

Skills:

Spelling Words with **ou** and **ow**

Spelling Theme Vocabulary

Visual Memory

Spelling Practice

Read and Spell	Copy and Spell	Spell It Again!
1. town	____________	____________
2. found	____________	____________
3. about	____________	____________
4. house	____________	____________
5. group	____________	____________
6. country	____________	____________
7. around	____________	____________
8. bridge	____________	____________
9. tower	____________	____________
10. park	____________	____________

Rhyme Time

Skills:

Rhyming Words

Finish the second line for each poem. Use a spelling word that rhymes with the word in color.

Example: She dropped a pink **flower**,
From the top of the **tower**.

The tiny gray **mouse**,
Lived under our ________________.

We heard Barney's lonely **bark**,
All the way across the ________________.

I bought an ice-cream **scoop**,
For all the children in our ________________.

We looked up, and we looked **down**,
We searched around the entire ________________.

We drove along the **ridge**,
Then we came to a high orange ________________.

Skills:

Spelling Words with **ou** and **ow**

Spelling Theme Vocabulary

Auditory Discrimination

Using Context Clues to Find Missing Words

Sound Search

Underline the words with the sound ow as in clown. Then circle the letters that make the sound.

found	about	park	tower	house
bridge	town	group	country	around

Write the correct words to complete each sentence.

1. Have you ____________ the president's ____________?

   about house group found

   ____

2. This ____________ crosses over to the ____________.

   found around park bridge

   ____

3. Our tour ____________ climbed up the ____________.

   group house country tower

   ____

4. I learned a lot ____________ my ____________.

   country about found bridge

   ____

5. There is much to see ____________ this ____________.

   group town around found

   ____

Capital City

Skills:

Using Capital Letters Correctly

Writing Complete Sentences

Use a capital letter to begin:

- the first word of a sentence
- the names of days, months, and holidays
- the word that names yourself—I
- names of people, pets, and special places
- people's titles

Circle the letters that should be capitalized.

1. josh wants to visit the grand canyon next year.

____

2. dr. march lectured about washington, d.c.

____

3. on saturday, we will visit the lincoln memorial.

____

4. tanya brought her dog fuzzy to lincoln park.

____

5. min and i had a barbeque on labor day.

____

6. mr. kahn gave us a tour of huntington library.

____

Skills:

Writing a Poem

Poetry Time

Create a poem. Write a word or phrase that starts with each letter in the topic word. Use the words in the story to help you.

V ______________________________

A ______________________________

C ______________________________

A ______________________________

T ______________________________

I ______________________________

O ______________________________

N ______________________________

Spellamadoodle

Skills:

Writing Spelling Words

Write each spelling word on the outline of the drawing. You may use the words more than once. For fun, decorate the drawing.

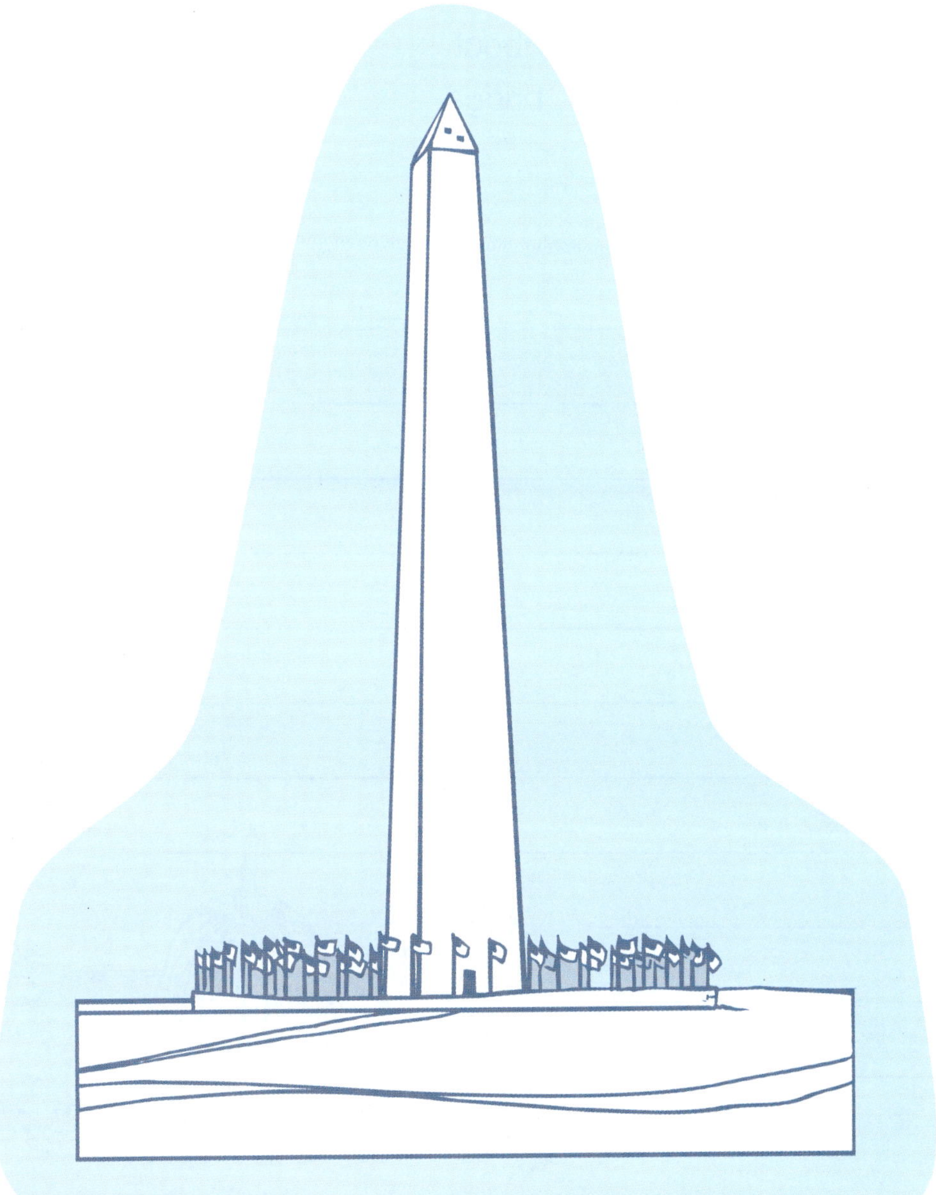

town	found	about	house	group
country	around	bridge	tower	park

Skills:

Writing a Journal Entry

My Favorite Place

Think of a favorite place you've visited. What did you like about it? What do you remember about your trip? Write a journal entry below about one day on your trip. Use as many spelling words as you can.

town	found	about	house	group
country	around	bridge	tower	park

Check Your Writing

- ◯ I used a capital letter at the beginning of each sentence and for each proper noun.
- ◯ I checked my spelling.

Special Vacation

Skills:

Using Context Clues to Find Missing Words

Use the spelling words to complete these paragraphs.

I have ____________ so many interesting cities to visit in our ____________. One interesting city is San Francisco, California. This city has many landmarks. The Golden Gate Bridge is very famous. The huge orange ____________ crosses the bay.

The bridge is near Golden Gate Park. This is a huge ____________ where people can visit the Japanese Tea Garden. A ____________ of my friends live in a ____________ near the park. They like to jog ____________ the park.

Another landmark is Coit Tower. This ____________ was built to honor the city's firefighters. There are so many interesting things to see and do in San Francisco. I've often thought ____________ moving there myself.

town	found	about	house	group
country	around	bridge	tower	park

TEST YOUR SKILLS

Washington, D.C.

Find the correct answer. Fill in the circle.

1. Which sentence has correct capital letters?
   - ❍ Mrs. Quinn showed us the Boston Museum of Art.
   - ❍ Mrs. quinn showed us the boston Museum of art.
   - ❍ mrs. Quinn showed us the Boston museum of art.

2. Which sentence has correct capital letters?
   - ❍ jesse and I went to san francisco, california.
   - ❍ Jesse and I went to San Francisco, California.
   - ❍ Jesse and i went to san francisco, california.

3. Which word is spelled correctly?
   - ❍ tower
   - ❍ towur
   - ❍ touer

4. Which word means "a part of the world with its own borders and government"?
   - ❍ bridge
   - ❍ town
   - ❍ country

My Spelling Test

Ask someone to test you on the spelling words.

1. ______
2. ______
3. ______
4. ______
5. ______
6. ______
7. ______
8. ______
9. ______
10. ______

5. Write the sentence correctly.

our growp crossed Lily Bridge on the tour arrownd toun

______

______

In the Pond

It's April. It's spring. Time for all the baby animals to come out to play. Quiet! Look over there in the pond. Can you see the ducklings? There are six newborn babies following their mother. The little ducklings are learning how to swim. Mother duck knows how to raise her babies. She shows them where to find delicious duckweed. She also shows them how to dive. Watch those curious ducklings dive among the pond plants. Splash! Splash! A beautiful white swan swims to its nest, and a tiny brown tadpole wiggles to safety. Finally, the baby ducklings waddle home behind their mother. They are going back to their nest. The pond is quiet again.

Find It! Read the spelling words.
Check off the words you can find in the story.

- [ ] April
- [ ] babies
- [ ] over
- [ ] tiny
- [ ] raise
- [ ] white
- [ ] those
- [ ] duckweed
- [ ] duckling
- [ ] tadpole

How many spelling words did you find? ______

Skills:

Spelling Words with Long **a** and Long **i**

Spelling Theme Vocabulary

Visual Memory

Spelling Practice

Read and Spell	Copy and Spell	Spell It Again!
1. April	__________	__________
2. babies	__________	__________
3. over	__________	__________
4. tiny	__________	__________
5. raise	__________	__________
6. white	__________	__________
7. those	__________	__________
8. duckweed	__________	__________
9. duckling	__________	__________
10. tadpole	__________	__________

Word Search

Find and circle the spelling words in this word search. Words can go across, down, or diagonally.

W E A L K D U C E S R
I L N D U C K L I N G
B A E C K Y O U B E D
A H T S A P R I L O U
B W E P D U A K U D C
I S H A E B I T O O K
E Y T I N Y S F V J W
S A F E T Y E E S U E
O T H O S E R N I P E
W E U L M T P B S E D

Skills:

Spelling Words with Long **a** and Long **i**

Spelling Theme Vocabulary

Skills:

Spelling Words with Long **a** and Long **i**

Spelling Theme Vocabulary

Visual Memory

Scrambled Words

Unscramble each spelling word and match it to the correct spelling.

isabbe	white
tehiw	April
pAirl	babies
ckgidlnu	duckweed
irsae	tadpole
ytni	duckling
ekwedcud	those
orev	tiny
sehot	over
dotlepa	raise

Awesome Adjectives

Adjectives are words that describe nouns or pronouns.

- An adjective can tell what kind: old house
- An adjective can tell which one: that town
- An adjective can tell how many: two ponds

For each noun, write an adjective that tells what kind.

________________ joke	________________ duckling
________________ pond	________________ sweater

For each noun, write an adjective that tells which one.

________________ swan	________________ fish
________________ park	________________ shoes

For each noun, write an adjective that tells how many.

________________ tadpoles	________________ feathers
________________ babies	________________ books

Skills:

Identifying Kinds of Adjectives

Identifying and Using Adjectives

Skills:

Auditory Discrimination

Spelling Words with Long **a** and Long **i**

Spelling Theme Vocabulary

Visual Memory

Word Study

Fill in the missing letters to make spelling words.

tadp ___ ___e	th ___ s ___	wh ___ t ___
duckw ___ ___ d	r ___ ___ se	d ___ ___ kling

b ___ ___ ies	___ v ___ r	___ ___ ril	t ___ ___ y

Circle the words with the sound a as in bake. Underline the words with the sound i as in smile. Cross out the words with a different sound.

babies duckling tadpole

white those duckweed

tiny over April raise

Spellamadoodle

Write each spelling word on the outline of the drawing. You may use the words more than once. For fun, decorate the drawing.

April	babies	over	tiny	raise
white	those	duckweed	duckling	tadpole

Skills:

Writing Spelling Words

Skills:

Writing a Creative Story

Lost Animal Baby

Pretend you are an animal baby that has gotten separated from its mother. You could be a duckling lost in the tall grasses, or a tadpole fleeing from a hungry swan. What happens to you? Who do you meet? How do you find your mother? Write about it below. Use as many spelling words as you can.

April	babies	over	tiny	raise
white	those	duckweed	duckling	tadpole

Mothers and Babies

Skills:

Writing Information

Mother animals care for their babies in special ways. Mother ducks teach their babies to swim and find food. Mother frogs produce eggs and swim away. Mother swans teach their cygnets to fly. Choose one animal. Then write about how the mother cares for her babies.

Check Your Writing

- ◯ I used complete sentences.
- ◯ I used correct ending punctuation.
- ◯ I checked my spelling.

TEST YOUR SKILLS

In the Pond

Find the correct answer. Fill in the circle.

1. Which underlined word is an adjective?
   - ○ Tiny tadpoles fill the pond.
   - ○ We took pictures of the ducklings.
   - ○ The ducklings look lost.

2. Which underlined word is an adjective?
   - ○ The tadpoles disappeared.
   - ○ The white swan swam fast.
   - ○ The ducklings learned how to swim.

3. Which word is spelled correctly?
   - ○ rayse
   - ○ raize
   - ○ raise

4. Which word means "very small"?
   - ○ tiny
   - ○ tadpole
   - ○ babies

My Spelling Test

Ask someone to test you on the spelling words.

1. ____________________
2. ____________________
3. ____________________
4. ____________________
5. ____________________
6. ____________________
7. ____________________
8. ____________________
9. ____________________
10. ____________________

5. Write the sentence correctly.

can thoz wite duck babys find the pond

____

____

Zoo Quiz

Is your favorite animal at the zoo
Smarter than an elephant?
Smarter than you?
More useful than a monkey
Or a chimpanzee or two?
More fearless than a lion?
More careless than a kangaroo?
Which one is the happiest?
The snake? The bear? The gnu?
Which one is the funniest?
Or fastest at the zoo?
I think I like the tiger.
Do you have a favorite, too?
Tell me, yes, please do!

Find It! Read the spelling words.
Check off the words you can find in the story.

- [ ] useful
- [ ] smarter
- [ ] fastest
- [ ] funniest
- [ ] happiest
- [ ] fearless
- [ ] careless
- [ ] feed
- [ ] clean
- [ ] animal

How many spelling words did you find? ______

Skills:

Spelling Words with Suffixes **–ful**, **–er**, **–est**, **–less**

Spelling Theme Vocabulary

Visual Memory

Spelling Practice

Read and Spell	Copy and Spell	Spell It Again!
1. useful		
2. smarter		
3. fastest		
4. funniest		
5. happiest		
6. fearless		
7. careless		
8. feed		
9. clean		
10. animal		

Find the Words

Write the missing words to complete the sentences.

1. Do you think cheetahs are ______________ or ______________?

   animal fastest happiest feed

2. Zookeepers ______________ and ______________ the animals.

   fearless useful feed clean

3. The lion is said to be a ______________ ______________.

   animal funniest fearless fastest

4. I think elephants are ______________ than zebras.

   useful clean smarter careless

5. Many animals are ______________ to humans.

   happiest smarter feed useful

6. Monkeys are the ______________ animals in the zoo!

   feed clean funniest animal

Skills:

Spelling Words with Suffixes **–ful**, **–er**, **–est**, **–less**

Spelling Theme Vocabulary

Using Context Clues to Find Missing Words

Skills:

Spelling Words with Suffixes **–ful, –er, –est, –less**

Spelling Theme Vocabulary

Matching Words with Their Meanings

What Does It Mean?

Look at the meanings of the suffixes in the box. Then write the spelling word for each definition.

less = without	ful = full of	er = more	est = most

useful	smarter	fastest	funniest	happiest
fearless	careless	feed	clean	animal

1. more intelligent ______________________
2. most happy ______________________
3. without care ______________________
4. most fast ______________________
5. full of use ______________________
6. without fear ______________________
7. most funny ______________________

Comparing Words

An adjective tells about a noun. An adjective can make comparisons.

- Use er to compare two people, places, or things.

Elephants are taller than zebras.

- Use est to compare three or more people, places, or things.

Giraffes are the tallest animals in the zoo.

Skills:

Using Comparative and Superlative Adjectives

Write the correct adjective in the blank.

1. The zookeeper is the _____________ person in the zoo.
   smarter smartest

2. The green snakes are _____________ than the striped snakes.
   longer longest

3. The toucan has _____________ feathers than the flamingo.
   brighter brightest

4. Simba the lion is the _____________ in his pride.
   larger largest

5. That is the _____________ roar I've ever heard!
   louder loudest

6. Champ the chimp is the _____________ monkey here.
   older oldest

Skills:

Matching Words with Their Meanings

Make a Match

Write the letter of the definition next to the word.

_____	1. useful	a. not paying close attention
_____	2. fearless	b. to give food to
_____	3. smarter	c. causing the most laughter
_____	4. careless	d. free from dirt
_____	5. fastest	e. helpful
_____	6. feed	f. a living thing that is not a plant
_____	7. funniest	g. most cheerful
_____	8. clean	h. unafraid
_____	9. happiest	i. more intelligent or clever
_____	10. animal	j. moving the quickest

Spellamadoodle

Skills:

Writing
Spelling Words

Write each spelling word on the outline of the drawing. You may use the words more than once. For fun, decorate the drawing.

useful	smarter	fastest	funniest	happiest
fearless	careless	feed	clean	animal

Skills:

Answering Questions

Zoo Questions

Use words from "Zoo Quiz" to answer these questions about zoo animals.

1. Which zoo animal do you think is smart?

2. Which zoo animal do you think is fearless?

3. Which zoo animal do you think is fast?

4. Which zoo animal do you think is funny?

5. Which zoo animal do you think is useful?

Backyard Zoo

Skills:

Writing a Description

The zookeeper said you could bring home three animals from the zoo! Which animals would you choose? Describe how you would keep and care for them. Use some of the spelling words.

useful	smarter	fastest	funniest	happiest
fearless	careless	feed	clean	animal

✓ Check Your Writing

- ❍ I used complete sentences.
- ❍ I used commas correctly.
- ❍ I checked my spelling.

TEST YOUR SKILLS

Zoo Quiz

Find the correct answer. Fill in the circle.

1. Which adjective correctly completes this sentence?

   Jenny's cat is _____ than her dog.

   ❍ fluffy
   ❍ fluffier
   ❍ fluffiest

2. Which adjective correctly completes this sentence?

   Which giraffe's neck is the _____ in the group?

   ❍ long
   ❍ longer
   ❍ longest

3. Which word is spelled correctly?

   ❍ happyest
   ❍ happiess
   ❍ happiest

4. Which word means "free from dirt"?

   ❍ clean
   ❍ feed
   ❍ useful

My Spelling Test

Ask someone to test you on the spelling words.

1. ______________________
2. ______________________
3. ______________________
4. ______________________
5. ______________________
6. ______________________
7. ______________________
8. ______________________
9. ______________________
10. ______________________

5. Write the sentence correctly.

   i think the feerliss lion is a smarttr annimul than the zebra

   ____

   ____

Breakfast Is Served

On Saturday morning, my older brother Chris and I got up early. We wanted to make a surprise breakfast for our mother. I helped measure the milk, and then Chris showed me how to break the eggs. We cut up some bread cubes and put them in a baking dish. We poured the milk and eggs over the bread, and I sprinkled on some cheese. Then it was time for baking. I put it in the oven for twenty minutes. When Mom heard the timer go off, she came into the kitchen. Was she surprised to find a delicious breakfast ready to eat!

Find It!

Read the spelling words.
Check off the words you can find in the story.

- [ ] early
- [ ] heard
- [ ] friend
- [ ] eat
- [ ] measure
- [ ] break
- [ ] brother
- [ ] mother
- [ ] bread
- [ ] oven

How many spelling words did you find? ______

Skills:

Spelling Words with **ea**

Spelling Theme Vocabulary

Visual Memory

Spelling Practice

Read and Spell	Copy and Spell	Spell It Again!
1. early	__________	__________
2. heard	__________	__________
3. friend	__________	__________
4. eat	__________	__________
5. measure	__________	__________
6. break	__________	__________
7. brother	__________	__________
8. mother	__________	__________
9. bread	__________	__________
10. oven	__________	__________

Spell It

Circle the word in each row that is spelled correctly.

1.	hurd	heard	herde
2.	ovven	ovun	oven
3.	muther	mother	mothre
4.	friend	frend	freind
5.	eat	eet	eate
6.	erly	urley	early
7.	mesurre	measure	meassur
8.	brother	bruther	broethr
9.	brak	breek	break
10.	bread	brede	breadd

Skills:

Spelling Words with **ea**

Spelling Theme Vocabulary

Visual Memory

Skills:

Spelling Words with **ea**

Spelling Theme Vocabulary

Matching Words with Their Meanings

Crossword Challenge

Complete the crossword puzzle using the spelling words.

early	heard	friend	eat	measure
break	brother	mother	bread	oven

Down

1. a boy or man who has the same parents as another person
2. to have sensed sounds through your ears
4. a baked food made from flour, water, and often yeast
5. an enclosed space where food is baked or roasted
6. a female parent
7. before the usual time

Across

3. someone whom you know well and enjoy being with
6. to find out the size, capacity, or weight of something
8. to take in food through the mouth
9. to damage something so that it is in pieces

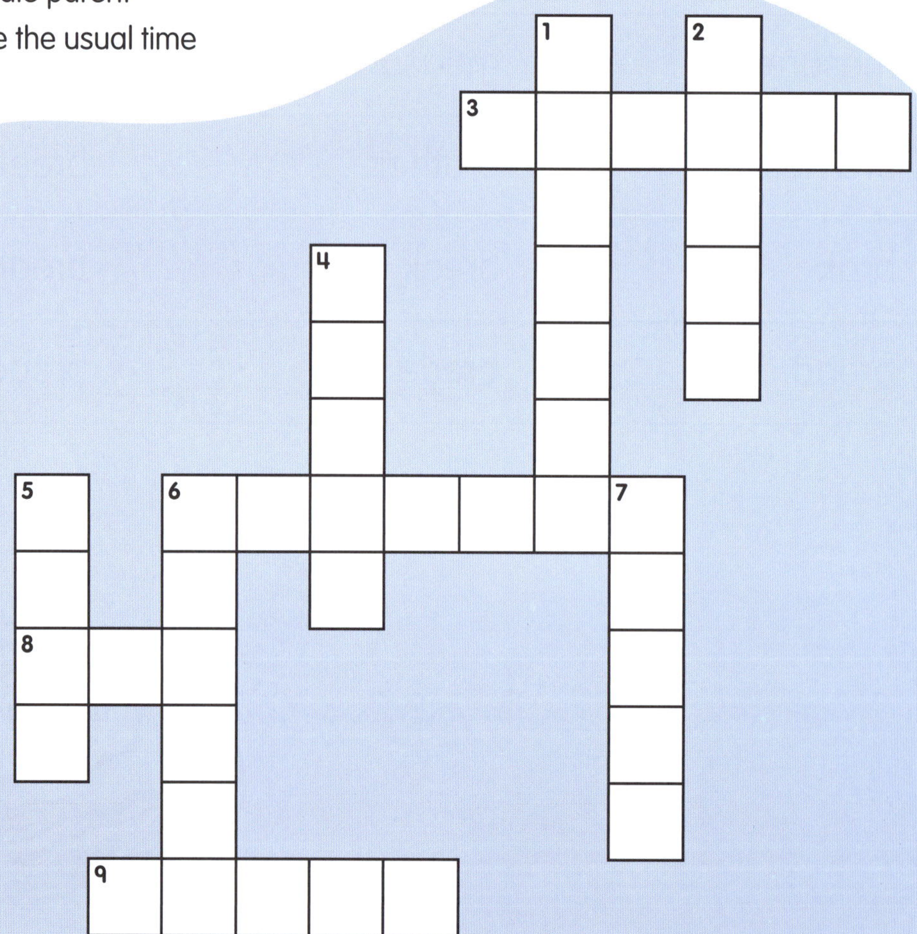

Action and Helping Verbs

Skills:

Identifying and Using Action and Helping Verbs

A **verb** tells what is happening to the noun.

- **Action verbs** show an action.

measure, cook, break, eat

- **Helping verbs** come before the main verb to tell about the action.

will, has, had, have, could, would, should, do, does, did

Write the correct verb in the blank. Then write **A** for **action** or **H** for **helping** in the box after the sentence.

1. In the morning, I ____________ the warm sun on my face.
   sleep would feel

2. Let's ____________ breakfast for Mother.
   make should am

3. I know he ____________ snooze and snore.
   was have will

4. Eggs and bacon ____________ in the pan.
   sizzle am will

5. We ____________ make tasty pancakes, too.
   does could is

Skills:

Auditory Discrimination

Visual Memory

Word Study

Say each word aloud. Then write it next to the correct sound.

heard measure eat bread break early

1. **a** as in **bake**	________	
2. **e** as in **bed**	________	________
3. **ir** as in **bird**	________	________
4. **e** as in **weak**	________	

Fill in the missing letters.

1. br ___ th ___ ___
2. fr ___ ___ nd
3. m ___ th ___ ___
4. ___ v ___ n

Spellamadoodle

Write each spelling word on the outline of the drawing. You may use the words more than once. For fun, decorate the drawing.

early	heard	friend	eat	measure
break	brother	mother	bread	oven

Skills:

Writing Spelling Words

Skills:

Writing a Recipe

My Favorite Recipe

What is a favorite food that you can make yourself? Write your favorite recipe below. Remember to write the steps in order.

Recipe for: ____________________

You will need:

____________________ ____________________

____________________ ____________________

____________________ ____________________

1. ____________________
____
2. ____________________
____
3. ____________________
____
4. ____________________
____
5. ____________________
____
6. ____________________
____

Special Gift

Skills:

Writing a Personal Narrative

The children in the story are making a special breakfast for their mother. What special gifts have you received? Write about a time when someone gave you a wonderful gift.

Check Your Writing

- ◯ I wrote complete sentences.
- ◯ I used correct punctuation.
- ◯ I checked my spelling.

TEST YOUR SKILLS

Breakfast Is Served

Find the correct answer. Fill in the circle.

1. In which sentence is the underlined word an action verb?
   - ◯ Shania is an excellent cook.
   - ◯ Shania has big dreams.
   - ◯ Shania bakes delicious pies.

2. In which sentence is the helping verb underlined?
   - ◯ Trey will make dinner tonight.
   - ◯ He likes steak and baked potatoes.
   - ◯ We brought the dessert.

3. Which word is spelled correctly?
   - ◯ meazhur
   - ◯ measure
   - ◯ meshure

4. Which word means "an enclosed space where food is baked"?
   - ◯ oven
   - ◯ eat
   - ◯ bread

My Spelling Test

Ask someone to test you on the spelling words.

1. ______________________
2. ______________________
3. ______________________
4. ______________________
5. ______________________
6. ______________________
7. ______________________
8. ______________________
9. ______________________
10. ______________________

5. Write the sentence correctly.

muthr's frends is coming eurly to bake bredd

____

____

Once upon a Time

Long, long ago, Princess Dahlia sat in her room in the castle. On this dreamy night, Dahlia thought about her future. She wished to be a squire, just like her brother. Then someday, she could become a knight! Dahlia loved each story about the knights' bravery as they brought peace to the land. Their skills in war were unmatched. Their adventures seemed endless. Dahlia longed to have her own adventures out there in the world. She closed her eyes to think what her life might be like. Suddenly, she felt something enter her room. When Dahlia opened her eyes, the room was full of golden light. She was dressed in a suit of shining armor! A shield was ready at her side. She was about to begin a new adventure!

Find It!

Read the spelling words.
Check off the words you can find in the story.

- [ ] war
- [ ] night
- [ ] knight
- [ ] piece
- [ ] peace
- [ ] their
- [ ] there
- [ ] castle
- [ ] story
- [ ] princess

How many spelling words did you find? ______

Skills:

Homophones

Spelling Theme Vocabulary

Visual Memory

Spelling Practice

Read and Spell	Copy and Spell	Spell It Again!
1. war		
2. night		
3. knight		
4. piece		
5. peace		
6. their		
7. there		
8. castle		
9. story		
10. princess		

Sound Search

Say the words in the box aloud. Write the two words that sound the same on the lines.

night	peace	there	wore
piece	their	war	knight

1.	______________________ ______________________	**3.**	______________________ ______________________
2.	______________________ ______________________	**4.**	______________________ ______________________

What spelling word means the opposite of _____?

war ____

here ____

day ____

What spelling word means the same as _____?

part ____

tale ____

belonging to them ________________________________

Skills:

Homophones

Spelling Theme Vocabulary

Synonyms and Antonyms

Skills:

Homophones

Spelling Theme Vocabulary

Visual Memory

Super Spellings

Circle the word that correctly completes each sentence.

1. It was a dark, starry knight/night.
2. The knight/night wore a suit of shining armor.
3. They spread peace/piece across the land.
4. A peace/piece of her dream came true.
5. She saw the shield their/there in the corner.
6. The knights gave their/there all to the war.

Circle the words that are spelled correctly.

peece	story	prinsces	cassle
castle	nitek	night	peace
wor	ther	war	princess
their	peice	there	night

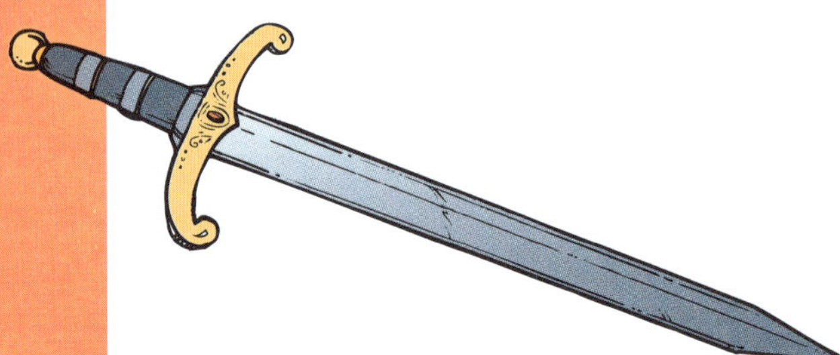

Correcting Capitals

Skills:

Using Capital Letters

Writing Complete Sentences

Correct the words that need capital letters. Cross out the small letter and write the capital letter above it.

july	morning	dr. barns
labor day	thursday	week
mr. gonzales	sister	brett
teacher	ms. spencer	halloween

Circle the letters that should be capitalized. Then rewrite the sentences.

1. at night, the princess dreamed of king william.

   ____

2. is saturday dahlia's favorite day of the week?

   ____

3. "i practice sword fighting on tuesdays," the knight said.

   ____

4. the gallant prince john rode the white steed.

   ____

5. "would you like to be a squire?" the fairy asked.

   ____

Skills:

Visual Sequencing

Recognizing Spelling Words

Word Search

Find and circle the spelling words. Words can go across, down, or diagonally.

war	night	knight	piece	peace
their	there	castle	story	princess

T	E	N	D	E	R	H	A	R	T	O	T
T	O	P	I	E	C	E	Z	H	A	N	D
H	H	E	R	U	G	S	G	O	T	D	N
E	O	G	H	I	P	I	N	O	L	D	A
I	B	S	I	S	N	O	R	A	Y	O	L
R	O	S	E	N	O	C	W	A	R	E	G
P	E	A	C	E	K	O	E	X	O	L	N
I	A	T	A	N	K	C	A	S	T	L	E
E	R	E	H	T	H	E	N	O	S	E	S

Spellamadoodle

Skills:

Writing Spelling Words

Write each spelling word on the outline of the drawing. You may use the words more than once. For fun, decorate the drawing.

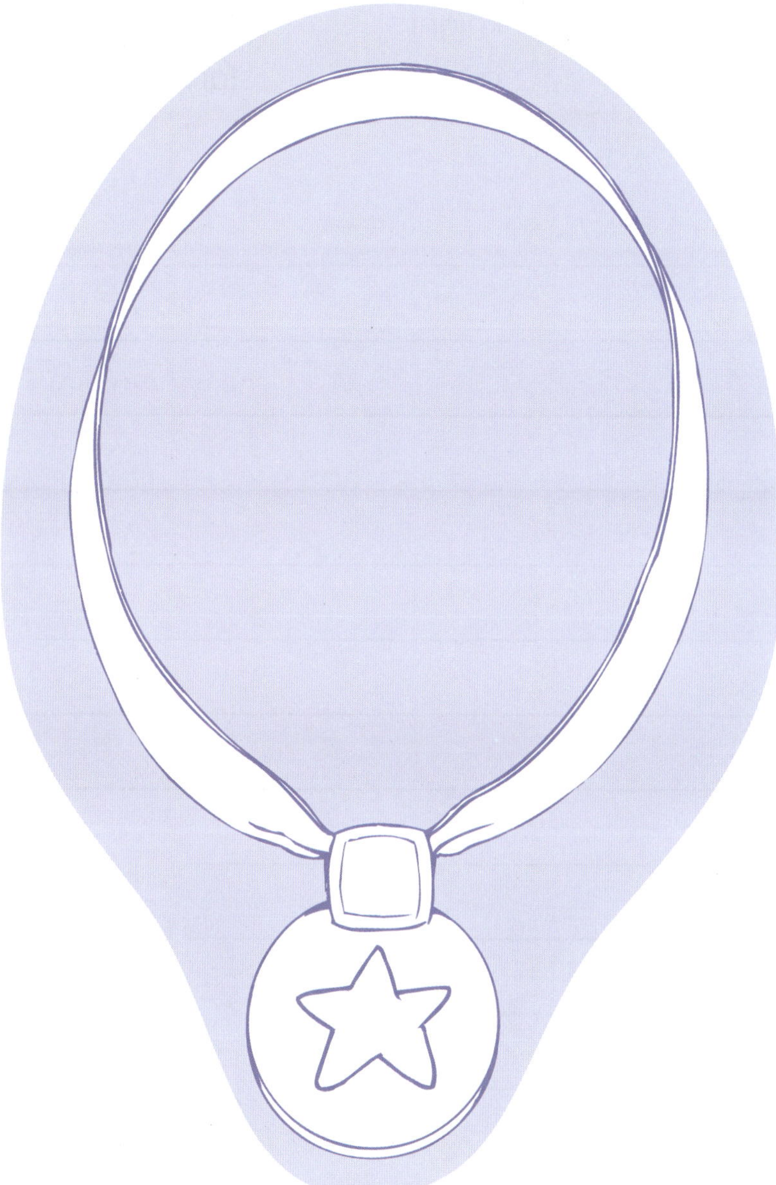

war	night	knight	piece	peace
their	there	castle	story	princess

Skills:

Writing a Fairy Tale

What Happened Next?

What do you think happened to Dahlia after she got her suit of armor and her shield? Write about her new adventures. Use as many spelling words as you can.

war	night	knight	piece	peace
their	there	castle	story	princess

Check Your Writing

- I used capital letters correctly.
- I wrote complete sentences.
- I checked my spelling.

The Perfect Knight

Skills:

Writing a List

Knights in the Middle Ages lived by a strict code. This code included rules about honor and bravery. What do you think are important skills for a knight to have? Strong? Polite? Brave? List eight skills below.

1. ______________________________

2. ______________________________

3. ______________________________

4. ______________________________

5. ______________________________

6. ______________________________

7. ______________________________

8. ______________________________

TEST YOUR SKILLS

Once upon a Time

Find the correct answer. Fill in the circle.

1. Which sentence has correct capital letters?
   - ◯ king george knighted james on Sunday.
   - ◯ King george Knighted James on sunday.
   - ◯ King George knighted James on Sunday.

2. Which sentence has correct capital letters?
   - ◯ dahlia wanted to be a knight for halloween.
   - ◯ Dahlia wanted to be a knight for halloween.
   - ◯ Dahlia wanted to be a knight for Halloween.

3. Which word is spelled correctly?
   - ◯ castle
   - ◯ cassle
   - ◯ cassel

4. Which word means "the time between sunset and sunrise"?
   - ◯ story
   - ◯ war
   - ◯ night

My Spelling Test

Ask someone to test you on the spelling words.

1. ______________________
2. ______________________
3. ______________________
4. ______________________
5. ______________________
6. ______________________
7. ______________________
8. ______________________
9. ______________________
10. ______________________

5. Write the sentence correctly.

the knite's storey of peese spread through the land

____

____

Postcard from Mexico

Dear Jordan,

Here is your postcard from Mexico. We are having a really fun vacation. The beach here is beautiful, and the sand is white like sugar. The air is so warm that we can wear our summer clothes, even at night! The people are friendly, too.

Yesterday we rented a sailboat. You should have seen the color of the ocean. It was bright blue, and we could see all the way to the bottom! The water was as warm as a bath. Every day, we eat all of our favorite Mexican foods. This is a vacation to remember. Wish you were here!

Your friend,
Ana

Find It!

Read the spelling words.
Check off the words you can find in the story.

- [ ] air
- [ ] beautiful
- [ ] vacation
- [ ] sailboat
- [ ] people
- [ ] favorite
- [ ] remember
- [ ] suitcase
- [ ] postcard
- [ ] clothes

How many spelling words did you find? ______

Skills:

Compound Words

Spelling Theme Vocabulary

Visual Memory

Spelling Practice

Read and Spell	Copy and Spell	Spell It Again!
1. air		
2. beautiful		
3. favorite		
4. clothes		
5. people		
6. vacation		
7. remember		
8. suitcase		
9. postcard		
10. sailboat		

Circle and Spell

Circle the word in each row that is spelled correctly.

1.	clothes	clothz	cloese
2.	sutecas	suitcase	sootcase
3.	butiful	beautiful	beutifull
4.	peeple	pepole	people
5.	air	aer	aire
6.	postkerd	posttcarde	postcard
7.	faverit	favorite	faverote
8.	remember	remmembr	rememmber
9.	salebote	saillboate	sailboat
10.	vacation	vakashion	vacasion

Skills:

Compound Words

Spelling Theme Vocabulary

Visual Memory

Skills:

Compound Words

Spelling Theme Vocabulary

Visual Memory

Building Words

Fill in the missing letters to make spelling words.

1.	b ___ ___ utif ___ l	6.	s ___ ___ tc ___ se
2.	cl ___ ___ ___ es	7.	p ___ ___ pl ___
3.	___ ___ r	8.	rem ___ ___ b ___ r
4.	fav ___ ___ ___ te	9.	postc ___ ___ ___
5.	s ___ ___ lbo ___ t	10.	vaca ___ ___ ___ n

Draw a line between the words to make compound spelling words. Write the words on the lines.

sail	card	____________________
suit	boat	____________________
post	case	____________________

Word Search

Find and circle the spelling words. Words can go across, down, or diagonally.

air	beautiful	favorite	clothes	people
vacation	remember	suitcase	postcard	sailboat

W	T	E	P	O	S	T	C	A	R	D	C
S	A	I	L	B	O	A	T	L	S	P	S
R	C	P	S	T	Q	E	U	H	Y	E	V
E	A	E	L	U	A	F	R	Y	H	I	A
F	A	V	O	R	I	T	E	T	D	E	C
R	U	I	A	T	R	T	O	I	L	R	A
I	E	W	U	H	Y	L	C	P	J	S	T
S	L	A	C	N	C	R	O	A	E	P	I
R	E	M	E	M	B	E	R	T	S	O	O
B	R	O	A	T	P	R	U	B	S	E	N

Skills:

Visual Sequencing

Recognizing Spelling Words

Skills:

Identifying and Using Past, Present, and Future Verb Tenses

Writing Complete Sentences

When Did It Happen?

A verb can show action. The tense of a verb tells when an action occurs.

- present—the action is happening now.

We are swimming.

- past—the action already happened.

I swam yesterday.

- future—the action is going to happen.

Tomorrow I will swim.

Rewrite this sentence in the present tense and then the past tense.

Tanya will write a postcard to her friend.

1. ______________________________

2. ______________________________

Rewrite this sentence in the past tense and then the future tense.

Marco feels the warm sand between his toes.

1. ______________________________

2. ______________________________

Rewrite this sentence in the present and then the future tense.

Jake and Kaitlin sailed on their vacation.

1. ______________________________

2. ______________________________

Spellamadoodle

Skills:

Writing Spelling Words

Write each spelling word on the outline of the drawing. You may use the words more than once. For fun, decorate the drawing.

air	beautiful	favorite	clothes	people
vacation	remember	suitcase	postcard	sailboat

Skills:

Writing a Postcard

Postcard to a Friend

What kinds of trips have you taken? Have you visited a museum, the zoo, or the beach? Write a postcard to a friend telling about your trip. Use as many spelling words as you can.

air	beautiful	favorite	clothes	people
vacation	remember	suitcase	postcard	sailboat

To:

Check Your Writing

- ❍ I used a capital letter to begin each sentence.
- ❍ I wrote complete sentences.
- ❍ I checked my spelling.

My Favorite Places

On the postcard, Ana describes Mexico to her friend. Think of three of your favorite places. Describe what you like about each place.

Favorite Place #1: ______________________

____

____

____

____

Favorite Place #2: ______________________

____

____

____

____

Favorite Place #3: ______________________

____

____

____

____

Skills:

Writing Descriptions

TEST YOUR SKILLS Postcard from Mexico

Find the correct answer. Fill in the circle.

1. Which tense is the verb in this sentence?

   Jordan will read his postcard after school.

   ❍ past
   ❍ present
   ❍ future

2. Which tense is the verb in this sentence?

   Ana travels to Mexico every summer.

   ❍ past
   ❍ present
   ❍ future

3. Which word is spelled correctly?

   ❍ sailboat
   ❍ sailbote
   ❍ saillboate

4. Which word means "the mixture of gases that surround the Earth"?

   ❍ people
   ❍ air
   ❍ beautiful

My Spelling Test

Ask someone to test you on the spelling words.

1. ____________________
2. ____________________
3. ____________________
4. ____________________
5. ____________________
6. ____________________
7. ____________________
8. ____________________
9. ____________________
10. ____________________

5. Write the sentence correctly.

   remumbr to bring your fovurit clothz

   ____

   ____

Test Your Skills–Record Form

Unit	Test Page	Topic	Test Your Skills Score (5 possible)	Spelling Test Score (10 possible)
1	12	Let's Go Camping!		
2	22	At the Library		
3	32	Sports, Sports, Sports		
4	42	Family Rap		
5	52	Mystery Map		
6	62	Money Matters		
7	72	Washington, D.C.		
8	82	In the Pond		
9	92	Zoo Quiz		
10	102	Breakfast Is Served		
11	112	Once upon a Time		
12	122	Postcard from Mexico		

Pull-out Spelling Lists

Use these lists to give spelling tests, post on the refrigerator, and for extra practice.

Unit 1 Let's Go Camping!	Unit 2 At the Library	Unit 3 Sports, Sports, Sports
1. pitch	1. next	1. point
2. drink	2. left	2. coach
3. swim	3. help	3. tie
4. which	4. please	4. everybody
5. light	5. believe	5. everyone
6. while	6. many	6. outside
7. find	7. between	7. basketball
8. fire	8. order	8. skateboard
9. tent	9. author	9. earthquake
10. camp	10. title	10. homework

Pull-out Spelling Lists

Use these lists to give spelling tests, post on the refrigerator, and for extra practice.

Unit 4 Family Rap	Unit 5 Mystery Map	Unit 6 Money Matters
1. I'm	1. letter	1. again
2. it's	2. different	2. given
3. they're	3. pattern	3. other
4. we're	4. middle	4. does
5. that's	5. Mississippi	5. some
6. o'clock	6. zipper	6. money
7. let's	7. carry	7. change
8. together	8. compass	8. read
9. home	9. backpack	9. bank
10. family	10. river	10. save

Pull-out Spelling Lists

Use these lists to give spelling tests, post on the refrigerator, and for extra practice.

Unit 7 Washington, D.C.	Unit 8 In the Pond	Unit 9 Zoo Quiz
1. town	1. April	1. useful
2. found	2. babies	2. smarter
3. about	3. over	3. fastest
4. house	4. tiny	4. funniest
5. group	5. raise	5. happiest
6. country	6. white	6. fearless
7. around	7. those	7. careless
8. bridge	8. duckweed	8. feed
9. tower	9. duckling	9. clean
10. park	10. tadpole	10. animal

Pull-out Spelling Lists

Use these lists to give spelling tests, post on the refrigerator, and for extra practice.

Unit 10 Breakfast Is Served	Unit 11 Once upon a Time	Unit 12 Postcard from Mexico
1. early	1. war	1. air
2. heard	2. night	2. beautiful
3. friend	3. knight	3. favorite
4. eat	4. piece	4. clothes
5. measure	5. peace	5. people
6. break	6. their	6. vacation
7. brother	7. there	7. remember
8. mother	8. castle	8. suitcase
9. bread	9. story	9. postcard
10. oven	10. princess	10. sailboat

Answer Key

Page 3

Let's Go Camping!

My family likes to camp in the mountains every summer. We find a good spot near the lake to pitch our tent. That makes it easy to swim whenever we like. My brother and I look for firewood while Mom and Dad set up camp. Then we light a big fire. My family tells stories around the fire until we can't stay awake any longer. The next day, we pack a lunch. We get water to drink. We have a new boat this year. It's bigger than our old boat. We can't wait to put our boat in the lake. We'll sail over to Pine Island to go exploring. I wonder what we'll find?

Find It! Read the spelling words. Check off the words you can find in the story.

✓ pitch ✓ drink ✓ swim ✓ while ✓ light
which ✓ find ✓ fire ✓ tent ✓ camp

How many spelling words did you find? 9

©2005 by Evan-Moor Corp. • EMC 4539 • Spell & Write UNIT 1 3

Page 5

Find the Words

Skills: Words with Long and Short i; Spelling Theme Vocabulary; Using Context Clues to Find Missing Words

Write the missing spelling words to complete the sentences.

1. Let's pitch our tent near the lake. (which, tent, pitch)
2. I can swim while you fish for dinner. (while, swim, tent)
3. We will light the fire to toast marshmallows. (pitch, fire, light)
4. Did you find a good place to camp? (drink, find, camp)
5. That drink which is sweet, tastes good! (which, tent, drink)

©2005 by Evan-Moor Corp. • EMC 4539 • Spell & Write UNIT 1 5

Page 6

Scrambled Words

Skills: Visual Memory and Discrimination

Unscramble each word and write it on the line. Then match it to the correct spelling.

1. difn	find	tent
2. elwhi	while	pitch
3. pihct	pitch	light
4. ntet	tent	which
5. gthli	light	drink
6. frei	fire	find
7. cpma	camp	swim
8. dirkn	drink	fire
9. chwih	which	camp
10. wims	swim	while

6 UNIT 1 Spell & Write • EMC 4539 • ©2005 by Evan-Moor Corp.

Page 7

Match the Meanings

Skills: Matching Words with Their Meanings

Write the letter of the definition next to the spelling word.

c	1. find	a. during the time that something else is happening
a	2. while	b. a portable shelter held up by poles
e	3. pitch	c. to come across something
b	4. tent	d. to move through the water using the arms and legs
i	5. light	e. to put up a tent
g	6. fire	f. to swallow liquid
h	7. camp	g. flames, heat, and light produced by burning
f	8. drink	h. to live or stay outdoors
d	9. swim	i. to start something burning
j	10. which	j. a particular one

©2005 by Evan-Moor Corp. • EMC 4539 • Spell & Write UNIT 1 7

Page 8

Naming Things

Skills: Identifying Proper and Common Nouns; Capitalizing Proper Nouns

Nouns name a person, place, or thing.

- Common nouns name any person, place, or thing. They do not begin with a capital letter.

sister doctor deer

- Proper nouns name a specific person, place, or thing. They begin with a capital letter.

Idaho Dr. Drake Lake Tahoe

Cross out any letter that should be a capital letter. Then write the capital letter above it.

1. mount whitney (M W)	8. brother
2. girl	9. austin (J)
3. forest ranger	10. pine tree
4. mr. thompson (M T)	11. pine island (P I)
5. camp shasta (C S)	12. blue jay
6. crystal lake (C L)	13. montana (M)
7. forest	14. waterfall

8 UNIT 1 Spell & Write • EMC 4539 • ©2005 by Evan-Moor Corp.

Page 10

What Should I Bring?

Skills: Writing a List

Pretend you are going camping with your family. There is a lake, hiking trails, and a lot of different animals. What will you bring? Make a list below.

My Camping Checklist
sleeping bag
swimsuit

Responses will vary.

10 UNIT 1 Spell & Write • EMC 4539 • ©2005 by Evan-Moor Corp.

Page 11

Dear Friend . . .

Skills: Writing a Postcard

You are on a camping trip with your family. Write a postcard to a friend. Tell your friend all about the fun things you are doing! Use as many spelling words as you can.

light tent fire pitch swim
find which camp while drink

Responses will vary.

To:

Check Your Writing
- I used a capital letter for each name.
- I checked my spelling.

©2005 by Evan-Moor Corp. • EMC 4539 • Spell & Write UNIT 1 11

Page 12

Test Your Skills: Let's Go Camping!

Find the correct answer. Fill in the circle.

1. Which sentence has the correct capital letters?
   - ● Ranger Moore showed us Rabbit Trail.
   - ○ My brother jake caught fish in Mirror lake.
   - ○ Camp Canoe is open all Summer long.
2. Which sentence has the correct capital letters?
   - ○ My Family hiked on Mt. red rock.
   - ● We visited Red Rock Museum today.
   - ○ We saw many Deer at Breezy meadow.
3. Which word is spelled correctly?
   - ● light
   - ○ lite
   - ○ lighte
4. Which word means "to discover or come across something"?
   - ○ pitch
   - ● find
   - ○ which

My Spelling Test

Ask someone to test you on the spelling words.

1.
2.
3.
4.
5.
6.
7.
8.
9.
10.

5. Write the sentence correctly.

dad can let us swum wille he lites the fire

Dad can let us swim while he lights the fire.

12 ASSESSMENT 1 Spell & Write • EMC 4539 • ©2005 by Evan-Moor Corp.

Page 13

At the Library

The new library opened this weekend, and Dad took us to see it. There were many new things to see inside. I believe there are thousands of new books. The children's room is amazing! One bench has two friendly bears sitting on it. You can sit between the bears and read a book. There are several computers, and someone is always there to help you. We took a tour and learned about the number system that keeps the books in order. It was easy for me to find my favorite author. We left after the tour, but Dad said we could go again next week.

Find It!
Read the spelling words.
Check off the words you can find in the story.

- [x] next
- [x] left
- [x] help
- [ ] please
- [x] believe
- [x] many
- [x] between
- [x] order
- [x] author
- [ ] title

How many spelling words did you find? 8

©2005 by Evan-Moor Corp. • EMC 4539 • Spell & Write UNIT 2 13

Page 15

Word Study

Skills: Spelling Words with Long and Short e; Spelling Theme Vocabulary; Auditory Discrimination

Read the words. Write them in the correct column. One word will be in both columns.

help, please, between, next, believe, left, many

Sound of e as in eat	Sound of e as in bed
many	many
please	left
between	help
believe	next

Circle the correctly spelled word in each row.

1. oredr **order** ordur
2. menny manny **many**
3. **author** other awther
4. pleese **please** pleez
5. **title** tiet tittel

©2005 by Evan-Moor Corp. • EMC 4539 • Spell & Write UNIT 2 15

Page 16

Spelling Words

Skills: Spelling Words with Long and Short e; Spelling Theme Vocabulary

Fill in the missing letters to make spelling words.

next, left, help, please, believe, many, between, order, author, title

1. pl e a se
2. l e ft
3. betw e e n
4. m a ny
5. n e xt
6. t i t le
7. o r der
8. h e lp
9. bel i e ve
10. a u thor

16 UNIT 2 Spell & Write • EMC 4539 • ©2005 by Evan-Moor Corp.

Page 17

Picking Pronouns

Skills: Replacing Nouns with Pronouns

A pronoun is a word that takes the place of one or more nouns.

Jenna works at the library. She works at the library.

Use the pronouns below to replace the underlined words. Write the pronouns on the line. You will use some pronouns more than once.

he she you it they them

1. I believe Tanya checked out that book already. she
2. You can find books on many shelves. them
3. Chad likes books about dinosaurs. them
4. My mom read aloud books to the children. She
5. Children can sit between the bears to read. They
6. Please help me look up titles on the computer. it
7. These books are in a certain order. They
8. Dad left us in the children's room to read. He

©2005 by Evan-Moor Corp. • EMC 4539 • Spell & Write UNIT 2 17

Page 18

Which Word?

Skills: Using Context Clues to Identify Missing Words

Write the missing words on the lines.

1. Margie chose her book next. (believe, next, help)
2. Trey is the author of this book. (many, please, author)
3. Can you read the title of this book? (title, between, many)
4. Dad will help us at the library. (help, author, title)
5. Jack sat between both bears on the bench. (please, next, between)
6. I found so many books at the new library. (many, please, author)
7. We left after the tour. (order, left, please)
8. I learned what order the books are in. (please, left, order)

18 UNIT 2 Spell & Write • EMC 4539 • ©2005 by Evan-Moor Corp.

Page 20

My Favorite Books

Skills: Writing a List; Writing Descriptions

Do you visit the library often? What are some of the books you've read? List the titles of your three favorite books. Then write what each book was about.

1. Title — Responses will vary.
2. Title
3. Title

20 UNIT 2 Spell & Write • EMC 4539 • ©2005 by Evan-Moor Corp.

Page 21

Library Visit

Skills: Writing a Personal Narrative

Have you been to the library? What do you like to do there? How do you find the books you want? Describe a trip to the library. Use as many spelling words as you can.

next, left, help, please, believe, many, between, order, author, title

Responses will vary.

Check Your Writing
- I used a capital letter to begin each sentence.
- I used a period to end each sentence.
- I checked my spelling.

©2005 by Evan-Moor Corp. • EMC 4539 • Spell & Write UNIT 2 21

Page 22

Test Your Skills: At the Library

Find the correct answer. Fill in the circle.

1. Which pronoun would you use to replace the word **Maria**?
   - ○ the
   - ● she
   - ○ they
2. Which pronoun would you use to replace **the computer**?
   - ○ she
   - ○ they
   - ● it
3. Which word is spelled correctly?
   - ● many
   - ○ meny
   - ○ manny
4. Which word means "the writer of a book, play, or poem"?
   - ○ title
   - ● author
   - ○ order
5. Write the sentence correctly.
   we belleves this titel is nekst for our author
   We believe this title is next for our author.

My Spelling Test

Ask someone to test you on the spelling words.

1. ___
2. ___
3. ___
4. ___
5. ___
6. ___
7. ___
8. ___
9. ___
10. ___

22 ASSESSMENT 2 Spell & Write • EMC 4539 • ©2005 by Evan-Moor Corp.

Page 23

Sports, Sports, Sports

Everyone in my family likes to play sports. My mom is the coach of my softball team. We are called the Eastside Earthquakes. We won our city championship last season.

My big brother has a skateboard. He takes it to Irvine Skateboard Park to practice. Sometimes my friends and I go to watch.

When we finish our homework, my sister and I like to play basketball outside. My dad put up a hoop in the driveway. Sometimes he plays, too. Each time you throw the ball into the basket, you get a point. The first one to get twenty-one points wins.

Almost everybody I know is on some kind of sports team. Sports are not only fun, but also great exercise. What's your favorite sport?

Find It! Read the spelling words. Check off the words you can find in the story.

✓ point ✓ coach ✓ everybody ✓ everyone ✓ basketball
tie ✓ outside ✓ skateboard ✓ earthquake ✓ homework

How many spelling words did you find? 9

©2005 by Evan-Moor Corp. • EMC 4539 • Spell & Write UNIT 3 23

Page 25

Two Words Make One

Skills: Compound Words, Spelling, Theme Vocabulary, Visual Memory

Draw a line between two words to make compound spelling words.

basket — ball
earth — quake
out — side
home — work
every — body
skate — board
every — one

©2005 by Evan-Moor Corp. • EMC 4539 • Spell & Write UNIT 3 25

Page 26

Mini-Crosswords

Skills: Compound Words, Spelling, Theme Vocabulary

Complete the crossword puzzles using nine of the spelling words.

point coach tie everybody everyone
outside basketball skateboard earthquake homework

1. basketball (down); skateboard (across); outside (down)
2. everybody (across); coach (down)
3. homework (across); everyone (down); point (across); tie (across)

26 UNIT 3 Spell & Write • EMC 4539 • ©2005 by Evan-Moor Corp.

Page 27

Which Part Is It?

Skills: Identifying Subjects and Predicates

Every complete sentence has two parts.

- A subject is the part that names the main person, place, or thing.
- A predicate is the part that tells what the subject is or does.

(My mom) <u>bought me a basketball.</u>

Circle the subject and underline the predicate.

1. (My brother) <u>rides his skateboard at the park.</u>
2. (Our softball team) <u>won the championship.</u>
3. (Each player) <u>had several turns at bat.</u>
4. (Staci) <u>hit a home run in the sixth inning.</u>
5. (My whole family) <u>plays sports together.</u>

©2005 by Evan-Moor Corp. • EMC 4539 • Spell & Write UNIT 3 27

Page 28

Make a Match

Skills: Matching Words with Their Meanings

Write the letter of the definition next to the word.

e	1. point	a.	one who trains a sports team
i	2. outside	b.	sudden violent shaking of the earth
a	3. coach	c.	board with wheels that you stand on and ride
g	4. basketball	d.	each and every person
h	5. tie	e.	unit for scoring in a game
c	6. skateboard	f.	schoolwork done at home
d	7. everyone/everybody	g.	game played by 2 teams of 5 players each
b	8. earthquake	h.	when 2 teams have the same score
f	9. homework	i.	out of a building, or in the open air

28 UNIT 3 Spell & Write • EMC 4539 • ©2005 by Evan-Moor Corp.

Page 30

My Favorite Sport

Skills: Writing an Opinion Paper

What is your favorite sport? Do you like team sports like baseball? Or do you like to play on your own, like tennis? Write about your favorite sport below. Describe what you like about it.

Responses will vary.

30 UNIT 3 Spell & Write • EMC 4539 • ©2005 by Evan-Moor Corp.

Page 31

The Great Game

Skills: Writing a Sports Story

Using your favorite sport, write about a great game. Write about what happened. Who were the teams? Who won? Tell about a game you actually saw or played, or make up a game. Use as many spelling words as you can.

point coach tie everybody everyone
outside basketball skateboard earthquake homework

Responses will vary.

Check Your Writing

- I used complete sentences.
- I used correct spelling.
- I used correct capitalization and punctuation.

©2005 by Evan-Moor Corp. • EMC 4539 • Spell & Write UNIT 3 31

Page 32

Test Your Skills: Sports, Sports, Sports

Find the correct answer. Fill in the circle.

1. In which sentence does the line separate the subject and the predicate?
   - ● Torey's coach / took the team to the state finals.
   - ○ Torey's / coach took the team to the state finals.
   - ○ Torey's coach took / the team to the state finals.
2. In which sentence does the line separate the subject and predicate?
   - ○ Michael played / soccer last year.
   - ● Michael / played soccer last year.
   - ○ Michael player soccer / last year.
3. Which word is spelled correctly?
   - ○ skatboarde
   - ○ skateborde
   - ● skateboard
4. Which word means "a situation when two teams have the same score"?
   - ● tie
   - ○ point
   - ○ river

My Spelling Test

Ask someone to test you on the spelling words.

1. ___
2. ___
3. ___
4. ___
5. ___
6. ___
7. ___
8. ___
9. ___
10. ___

5. Write the sentence correctly.

our coche told evrybody to play bassketball outside

Our coach told everybody to play basketball outside.

32 ASSESSMENT 3 Spell & Write • EMC 4539 • ©2005 by Evan-Moor Corp.

Page 33

Family Rap

People who love you,
People who share,
They're the ones
Who'll always care.
A family.

People together,
People who say,
"We're proud of you
In every way."
A family.

People who help you,
People who make
A home that's happy.
It's no mistake.
A family.

People who know you,
People who see
All that you are,
And all you can be.
A family.

Find It! Read the spelling words. Check off the words you can find in the story.

☐ I'm ☑ it's ☑ they're ☑ we're ☐ o'clock
☐ let's ☑ together ☑ home ☑ family ☑ that's

How many spelling words did you find? 7

©2005 by Evan-Moor Corp. • EMC 4539 • Spell & Write UNIT 4 33

Page 35

Match and Spell

Skills: Contractions; Spelling Theme Vocabulary; Visual Memory

Draw a line between the two words that make each contraction. Write the word on the line.

I'm they're we're let's it's that's

let	is	let's
they	are	they're
that	is	that's
I	are	I'm
we	us	we're
it	am	it's

©2005 by Evan-Moor Corp. • EMC 4539 • Spell & Write UNIT 4 35

Page 36

Spell It

Skills: Contractions; Spelling Theme Vocabulary; Visual Memory

Circle the correctly spelled word in each row.

1.	were'	(we're)	wee're
2.	hume	homme	(home)
3.	toogeter	(together)	tugethr
4.	(let's)	lett's	lets'
5.	(family)	fammile	famully
6.	thayre	they'er	(they're)
7.	oh'clock	(o'clock)	o'clocke
8.	tha'ts	thats'	(that's)
9.	(I'm)	I'am	I'me
10.	i'ts	its'	(it's)

36 UNIT 4 Spell & Write • EMC 4539 • ©2005 by Evan-Moor Corp.

Page 37

Contraction Action

Skills: Using Apostrophes to Make Contractions

Use an apostrophe (') when making a contraction. The apostrophe takes the place of the missing letter or letters.

let us — let's   I am — I'm

Cross out the letter or letters in each set of words to make a contraction. Replace the letter or letters with an apostrophe. Write the contraction on the line. The first one has been done for you.

1. we will — we'll
2. have not — haven't
3. I will — I'll
4. they are — they're
5. he is — he's
6. it is — it's
7. can not — can't
8. did not — didn't

©2005 by Evan-Moor Corp. • EMC 4539 • Spell & Write UNIT 4 37

Page 38

Circle It!

Skills: Visual Memory; Contractions

Circle the correct spelling.

1. Ime (I'm) going to my soccer game.
2. My famile (family) is coming to watch.
3. The game starts at four (o'clock) oklock.
4. (It's) Its going to be a good game.
5. Weer'e (We're) going out for pizza afterward.
6. They know (that's) that'ts my favorite food.

38 UNIT 4 Spell & Write • EMC 4539 • ©2005 by Evan-Moor Corp.

Page 40

Families Care

Skills: Writing a Poem

Write a poem using the letters in the word family. Think of all the ways your family cares for you. Then write something that starts with each letter in the word. Your poem does not have to rhyme.

Examples:
Feeds and clothes me
Always there for me

F Responses will vary.
A
M
I
L
Y

40 UNIT 4 Spell & Write • EMC 4539 • ©2005 by Evan-Moor Corp.

Page 41

My Family Is Special

Skills: Writing a Personal Narrative

What makes your family special? Do you share a special tradition, event, talent, or relative? Write about your family below. Use as many spelling words as you can.

I'm it's they're we're o'clock
let's together home family that's

Responses will vary.

Check Your Writing
○ I used a capital letter for each name.
○ I checked my spelling.

©2005 by Evan-Moor Corp. • EMC 4539 • Spell & Write UNIT 4 41

Page 42

Test Your Skills — Family Rap

Find the correct answer. Fill in the circle.

1. Which contraction is made up of the two underlined words?
Jenny does not want to leave her family.
○ don't
● doesn't
○ didn't

2. Which contraction is made up of the two underlined words?
Mando is not ready for his test.
○ won't
○ it's
● isn't

3. Which word is spelled correctly?
○ familly
● family
○ famly

4. Which word means "a place where you live or belong"?
● home
○ o'clock
○ it's

5. Write the sentence correctly.
letts get tugethr when theyre finished
Let's get together when they're finished.

My Spelling Test

Ask someone to test you on the spelling words.

1.
2.
3.
4.
5.
6.
7.
8.
9.
10.

42 ASSESSMENT 4 Spell & Write • EMC 4539 • ©2005 by Evan-Moor Corp.

Page 43

Mystery Map

I found an old map on the playground. The map shows a river. In the middle of the river are three islands. One of them looks different because it has a huge X on it. This is a mystery! I think it shows where a forgotten treasure is hidden. Maybe it's gold coins or jewels. Do you want to help me look for it? We need to find it before it disappears. Meet me at the tunnel near the playground. Bring your backpack with the zipper and a compass. We might have to carry something back. Get ready to solve the mystery!

Find It! Read the spelling words. Check off the words you can find in the story.

letter ✓ different pattern ✓ middle ✓ zipper
✓ carry Mississippi ✓ compass ✓ backpack ✓ river

How many spelling words did you find? 7

©2005 by Evan-Moor Corp. • EMC 4539 • Spell & Write UNIT 5 43

Page 45

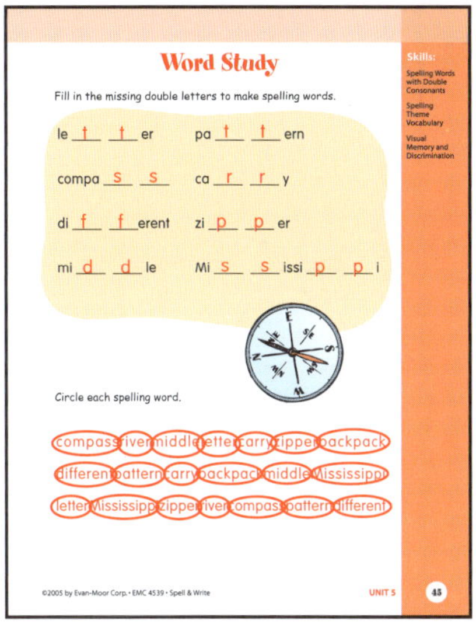

Word Study

Fill in the missing double letters to make spelling words.

le t t er pa t t ern
compa s s ca r r y
di f f erent zi p p er
mi d d le Mi s s issi p p i

Circle each spelling word.

compass river middle letter carry zipper backpack
different pattern carry backpack middle Mississippi
letter Mississippi zipper river compass pattern different

Skills: Spelling Words with Double Consonants; Spelling Theme Vocabulary; Visual Memory and Discrimination

©2005 by Evan-Moor Corp. • EMC 4539 • Spell & Write UNIT 5 45

Page 46

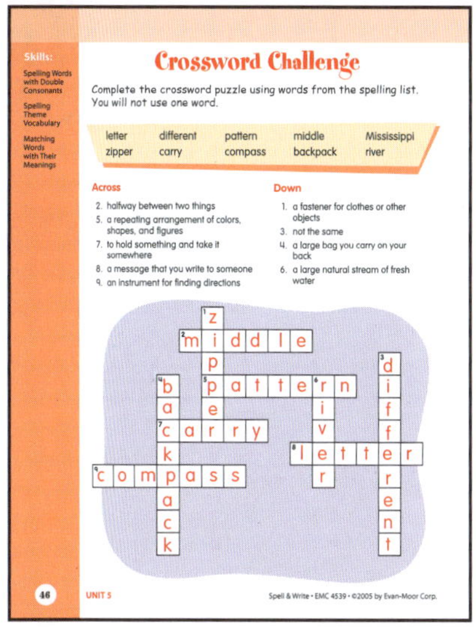

Crossword Challenge

Complete the crossword puzzle using words from the spelling list. You will not use one word.

letter different pattern middle Mississippi
zipper carry compass backpack river

Across
2. halfway between two things
5. a repeating arrangement of colors, shapes, and figures
7. to hold something and take it somewhere
8. a message that you write to someone
9. an instrument for finding directions

Down
1. a fastener for clothes or other objects
3. not the same
4. a large bag you carry on your back
6. a large natural stream of fresh water

Answers: middle, pattern, carry, letter, compass, zipper, different, backpack, river

Skills: Spelling Words with Double Consonants; Spelling Theme Vocabulary; Matching Words with Their Meanings

46 UNIT 5 Spell & Write • EMC 4539 • ©2005 by Evan-Moor Corp.

Page 47

Page 48

Page 50

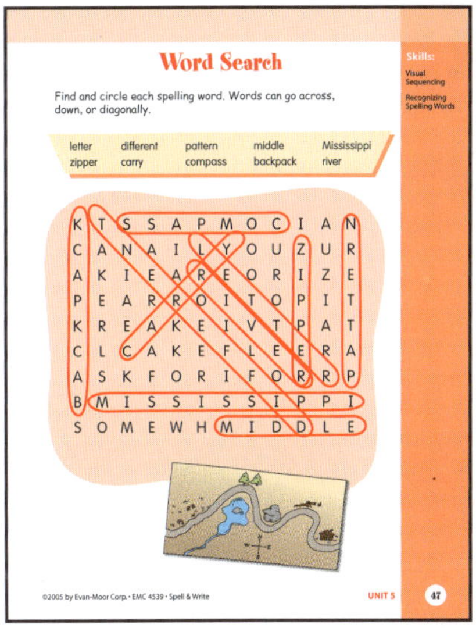

Word Search

Find and circle each spelling word. Words can go across, down, or diagonally.

letter different pattern middle Mississippi
zipper carry compass backpack river

Skills: Visual Sequencing; Recognizing Spelling Words

©2005 by Evan-Moor Corp. • EMC 4539 • Spell & Write UNIT 5 47

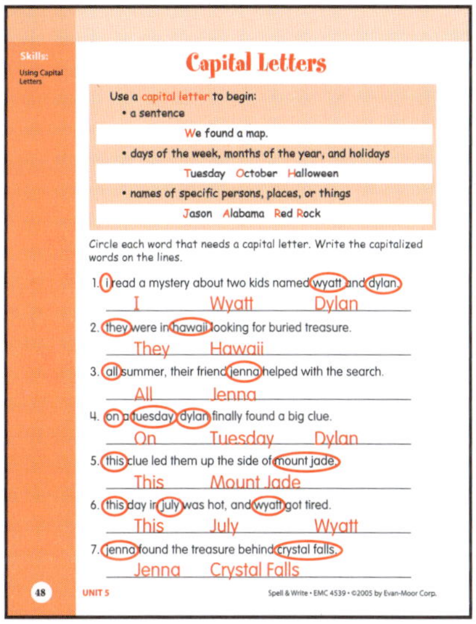

Capital Letters

Use a capital letter to begin:
• a sentence
We found a map.
• days of the week, months of the year, and holidays
Tuesday October Halloween
• names of specific persons, places, or things
Jason Alabama Red Rock

Circle each word that needs a capital letter. Write the capitalized words on the lines.

1. i read a mystery about two kids named wyatt and dylan. — I, Wyatt, Dylan
2. they were in hawaii looking for buried treasure. — They, Hawaii
3. all summer, their friend jenna helped with the search. — All, Jenna
4. on a tuesday dylan finally found a big clue. — On, Tuesday, Dylan
5. this clue led them up the side of mount jade. — This, Mount Jade
6. this day in july was hot, and wyatt got tired. — This, July, Wyatt
7. jenna found the treasure behind crystal falls. — Jenna, Crystal Falls

Skills: Using Capital Letters

48 UNIT 5 Spell & Write • EMC 4539 • ©2005 by Evan-Moor Corp.

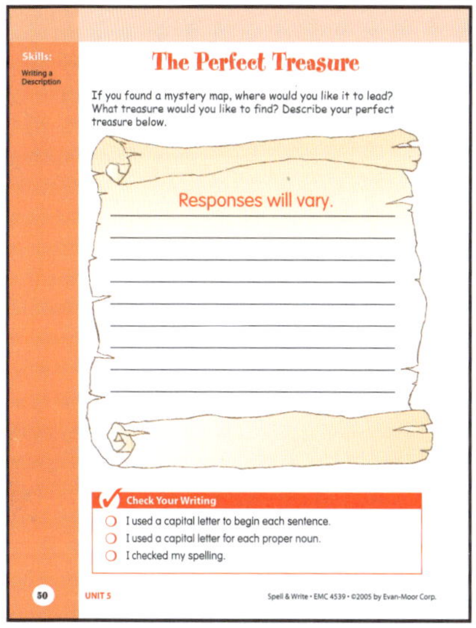

The Perfect Treasure

If you found a mystery map, where would you like it to lead? What treasure would you like to find? Describe your perfect treasure below.

Responses will vary.

Check Your Writing
I used a capital letter to begin each sentence.
I used a capital letter for each proper noun.
I checked my spelling.

Skills: Writing a Description

50 UNIT 5 Spell & Write • EMC 4539 • ©2005 by Evan-Moor Corp.

Page 51

Page 52

My Own Mystery Map

Think of a good place at school or in your neighborhood to hide buried treasure. Then write directions for how to find it! Draw a map to go with your directions below.

First,
Second,
Third, Responses will vary.
Then,
Next,
Last,

Skills: Writing Directions; Drawing a Map

©2005 by Evan-Moor Corp. • EMC 4539 • Spell & Write UNIT 5 51

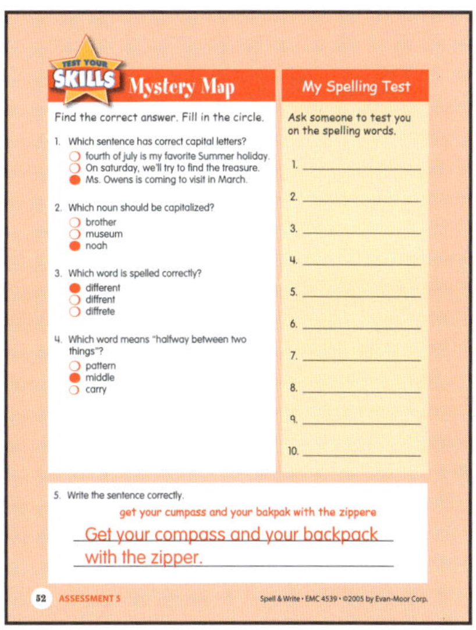

Test Your Skills: Mystery Map

Find the correct answer. Fill in the circle.

1. Which sentence has correct capital letters?
   - fourth of july is my favorite Summer holiday.
   - On saturday, we'll try to find the treasure.
   - ● Ms. Owens is coming to visit in March.
2. Which noun should be capitalized?
   - brother
   - museum
   - ● noah
3. Which word is spelled correctly?
   - ● different
   - diffrent
   - diffrete
4. Which word means "halfway between two things"?
   - pattern
   - ● middle
   - carry
5. Write the sentence correctly.
   get your compass and your bakpak with the zippere
   Get your compass and your backpack with the zipper.

My Spelling Test

Ask someone to test you on the spelling words.

1. 2. 3. 4. 5. 6. 7. 8. 9. 10.

52 ASSESSMENT 5 Spell & Write • EMC 4539 • ©2005 by Evan-Moor Corp.

Page 53

Money Matters

My grandpa is teaching me an important lesson—how to save my money. He has given me fifty dollars for my birthday every year. He takes me to the bank where I have an account. The bank teller puts the money in my account, and she writes the amount in my bankbook. Do you know what the bank does? It pays me for using my money!

Grandpa showed me how to save some money in a change jar, too. I put in quarters, dimes, nickels, and pennies. When the jar is full, I count the money. Then I put it into two piles. I keep one pile to spend, and I take the other to the bank. I like to read my bankbook. I can see my savings grow.

Find It! Read the spelling words. Check off the words you can find in the story.

again ✓given ✓other ✓does ✓some
✓money ✓change ✓read ✓bank ✓save

How many spelling words did you find? 9

©2005 by Evan-Moor Corp. • EMC 4539 • Spell & Write UNIT 6 53

Page 55

Word Study

Skills: Spelling Words with the Schwa Sound; Spelling Theme Vocabulary; Visual Memory; Auditory Discrimination

Circle the letter or letters in each word that make the sound of o in ton.

again does money
other some

Unscramble the letters to make spelling words. Write them on the lines.

1. igana again
2. eghacn change
3. vgein given
4. erhot other
5. nbka bank
6. vesa save
7. eosd does
8. yeonm money
9. edra read
10. moes some

©2005 by Evan-Moor Corp. • EMC 4539 • Spell & Write UNIT 6 55

Page 56

Write It Right

Skills: Spelling Words with the Schwa Sound; Spelling Theme Vocabulary; Visual Memory; Spelling in Context

Circle the misspelled words. Write them correctly on the lines.

1. Let's take our munny to the banck. money bank
2. Mom has givvan me sum coins. given some
3. Dous the teller help you make chanje? Does change
4. I can reade what I sav in my bankbook. read save
5. My uther piggy bank is full agane. other again

56 UNIT 6 Spell & Write • EMC 4539 • ©2005 by Evan-Moor Corp.

Page 57

Kinds of Sentences

Skills: Identifying Different Kinds of Sentences; Using Correct Ending Punctuation

There are four kinds of sentences. Each kind uses specific ending punctuation.

- A statement tells something. It ends with a period. (.)
- A question asks something. It ends with a question mark. (?)
- A command tells someone to do something. It ends with a period. (.)
- An exclamation shows strong feeling. It ends with an exclamation mark. (!)

Add the correct ending punctuation. Then write whether each sentence is a **statement, question, command,** or **exclamation**.

1. Did you count all your money ? question
2. Put your money in the bank . command
3. Wow, look at all that money ! exclamation
4. The bank is behind the library . statement
5. Who is the bank teller today ? question
6. My house is on fire ! exclamation
7. Did you save enough for a coat ? question
8. Count this change . command

©2005 by Evan-Moor Corp. • EMC 4539 • Spell & Write UNIT 6 57

Page 58

Make a Match

Skills: Matching Words with Their Meanings

Draw a line from each spelling word to its meaning.

again	one more time
given	to have handed something to another person
other	different, not the same
does	performing an action
some	an amount that is not named
money	coins and bills people use to buy things
change	coins, not bills
read	to look at written words and understand what they mean
bank	a place where people keep their money
save	to keep money to use in the future

58 UNIT 6 Spell & Write • EMC 4539 • ©2005 by Evan-Moor Corp.

Page 60

Lots of Money

Skills: Writing a List

You just won first place in a contest! You won $10,000! What are you going to do with the money? Buy presents? Save it in the bank? Go on a trip? List ten things you would do with the money.

1.
2. Responses will vary.
3.
4.
5.
6.
7.
8.
9.
10.

60 UNIT 6 Spell & Write • EMC 4539 • ©2005 by Evan-Moor Corp.

Page 61

Lost and Found

Skills: Writing a Creative Story

You've just found a wallet at the park. It's stuffed full of money! What will you do with it? Write your story below. Use as many spelling words as you can.

again given other does some
money change read bank save

Responses will vary.

Check Your Writing

- I used a capital letter to begin each sentence.
- I used correct punctuation at the end of each sentence.
- I checked my spelling.

©2005 by Evan-Moor Corp. • EMC 4539 • Spell & Write UNIT 6 61

Page 62

Test Your Skills: Money Matters

Find the correct answer. Fill in the circle.

1. What kind of sentence is this?
   Did you save your money in that jar?
   - statement
   - ● question
   - command
   - exclamation
2. What kind of sentence is this?
   Come with me to the bank
   - statement
   - question
   - ● command
   - exclamation
3. Which word is spelled correctly?
   - chanje
   - chainge
   - ● change
4. Which word means "different, not the same as mentioned"?
   - ● other
   - some
   - again
5. Write the sentence correctly.
   they have given me monny to savve in the banck
   They have given me money to save in the bank.

My Spelling Test

Ask someone to test you on the spelling words.

1.
2.
3.
4.
5.
6.
7.
8.
9.
10.

62 ASSESSMENT 6 Spell & Write • EMC 4539 • ©2005 by Evan-Moor Corp.

Page 63

Washington, D.C.

There are many places to see in Washington, D.C. This great city is the capital of the United States. We went with a group of people to see the White House. That is the house where the president lives. The White House was built in 1800! The address is 1600 Pennsylvania Avenue. Around town, there are many parks and museums to visit. We saw a tall white tower named after George Washington. It is called the Washington Monument. We also found a place where you can see airplanes and rockets. It is called the Smithsonian Institute. There are so many things to see in this city. I couldn't see everything. I hope that someday I can visit Washington, D.C., again.

Find It! Read the spelling words. Check off the words you can find in the story.

✓ town ✓ found about ✓ house ✓ group
✓ country ✓ around bridge ✓ tower ✓ park

How many spelling words did you find? 8

©2005 by Evan-Moor Corp. • EMC 4539 • Spell & Write UNIT 7 63

Page 65

Rhyme Time

Skills: Rhyming Words

Finish the second line for each poem. Use a spelling word that rhymes with the word in color.

Example: She dropped a pink flower,
From the top of the tower.

The tiny gray mouse,
Lived under our house

We heard Barney's lonely bark,
All the way across the park

I bought an ice-cream scoop,
For all the children in the our group

We looked up, and we looked down,
We searched around the entire town

We drove along the ridge,
Then we came to a high orange bridge

©2005 by Evan-Moor Corp. • EMC 4539 • Spell & Write UNIT 7 65

Page 66

Sound Search

Skills: Spelling Words with ou and ow; Spelling Theme Vocabulary; Auditory Discrimination; Using Context Clues to Find Missing Words

Underline the words with the sound ow as in clown. Then circle the letters that make the sound.

found about park tower house
bridge town group country around

Write the correct words to complete each sentence.

1. Have you found the president's house?
about house group found

2. This bridge crosses over to the park.
found around park bridge

3. Our tour group climbed up the tower.
group house country tower

4. I learned a lot about my country.
country about found bridge

5. There is much to see around this town.
group town around found

66 UNIT 7 Spell & Write • EMC 4539 • ©2005 by Evan-Moor Corp.

Page 67

Capital City

Skills: Using Capital Letters Correctly; Writing Complete Sentences

Use a capital letter to begin:
- the first word of a sentence
- the names of days, months, and holidays
- the word that names yourself—I
- names of people, pets, and special places
- people's titles

Circle the letters that should be capitalized.

1. josh wants to visit the grand canyon next year.
2. dr. march lectured about washington, d.c.
3. on saturday, we will visit the lincoln memorial.
4. tanya brought her dog fuzzy to lincoln park.
5. min and i had a barbeque on labor day.
6. mr. kahn gave us a tour of huntington library.

©2005 by Evan-Moor Corp. • EMC 4539 • Spell & Write UNIT 7 67

Page 68

Poetry Time

Skills: Writing a Poem

Create a poem. Write a word or phrase that starts with each letter in the topic word. Use the words in the story to help you.

V Responses will vary.
A
C
A
T
I
O
N

68 UNIT 7 Spell & Write • EMC 4539 • ©2005 by Evan-Moor Corp.

Page 70

My Favorite Place

Skills: Writing a Journal Entry

Think of a favorite place you've visited. What did you like about it? What do you remember about your trip? Write a journal entry below about one day on your trip. Use as many spelling words as you can.

town found about house group
country around bridge tower park

Responses will vary.

Check Your Writing
- I used a capital letter at the beginning of each sentence and for each proper noun.
- I checked my spelling.

70 UNIT 7 Spell & Write • EMC 4539 • ©2005 by Evan-Moor Corp.

Page 71

Special Vacation

Skills: Using Context Clues to Find Missing Words

Use the spelling words to complete these paragraphs.

I have found so many interesting cities to visit in our country. One interesting city is San Francisco, California. This city has many landmarks. The Golden Gate Bridge is very famous. The huge orange bridge crosses the bay.

The bridge is near Golden Gate Park. This is a huge park where people can visit the Japanese Tea Garden. A group of my friends live in a house near the park. They like to jog around the park.

Another landmark is Coit Tower. This tower was built to honor the city's firefighters. There are so many interesting things to see and do in San Francisco. I've often thought about moving there myself.

town found about house group
country around bridge tower park

©2005 by Evan-Moor Corp. • EMC 4539 • Spell & Write UNIT 7 71

Page 72

Test Your Skills: Washington, D.C.

Find the correct answer. Fill in the circle.

1. Which sentence has correct capital letters?
   - ● Mrs. Quinn showed us the Boston Museum of Art.
   - ○ Mrs. quinn showed us the boston Museum of art.
   - ○ mrs. Quinn showed us the Boston museum of art.
2. Which sentence has correct capital letters?
   - ○ jesse and I went to san francisco, california.
   - ● Jesse and I went to San Francisco, California.
   - ○ Jesse and i went to san francisco, california.
3. Which word is spelled correctly?
   - ● tower
   - ○ towur
   - ○ touer
4. Which word means "a part of the world with its own borders and government"?
   - ○ bridge
   - ○ town
   - ● country

5. Write the sentence correctly.
our growp crossed Lily Bridge on the tour arrownd toun
Our group crossed Lily Bridge on the tour around town.

My Spelling Test

Ask someone to test you on the spelling words.

1.
2.
3.
4.
5.
6.
7.
8.
9.
10.

72 ASSESSMENT 7 Spell & Write • EMC 4539 • ©2005 by Evan-Moor Corp.

Page 73

In the Pond

It's April. It's spring. Time for all the baby animals to come out to play. Quiet! Look over there in the pond. Can you see the ducklings? There are six newborn babies following their mother. The little ducklings are learning how to swim. Mother duck knows how to raise her babies. She shows them where to find delicious duckweed. She also shows them how to dive. Watch those curious ducklings dive among the pond plants. Splash! Splash! A beautiful white swan swims to its nest, and a tiny brown tadpole wiggles to safety. Finally, the baby ducklings waddle home behind their mother. They are going back to their nest. The pond is quiet again.

Find It! Read the spelling words. Check off the words you can find in the story.

- ✓ April ✓ babies ✓ over ✓ tiny ✓ raise
- ✓ white ✓ those ✓ duckweed ✓ duckling ✓ tadpole

How many spelling words did you find? 10

©2005 by Evan-Moor Corp. • EMC 4539 • Spell & Write UNIT 8 73

Page 75

Word Search

Skills: Spelling Words with Long a and Long i; Spelling Theme Vocabulary

Find and circle the spelling words in this word search. Words can go across, down, or diagonally.

W	E	A	L	K	D	U	C	E	S	R
I	L	N	D	U	C	K	L	I	N	G
B	A	E	C	K	Y	O	U	B	E	D
A	H	T	S	A	P	R	I	L	O	U
B	W	E	P	D	U	A	K	U	D	C
I	S	H	A	E	B	I	T	O	O	K
E	Y	T	I	N	Y	S	F	V	J	W
S	A	F	E	T	Y	E	E	S	U	E
O	T	H	O	S	E	R	N	I	P	E
W	E	U	L	M	T	P	B	S	E	D

©2005 by Evan-Moor Corp. • EMC 4539 • Spell & Write UNIT 8 75

Page 76

Scrambled Words

Skills: Spelling Words with Long a and Long i; Spelling Theme Vocabulary; Visual Memory

Unscramble each spelling word and match it to the correct spelling.

isabbe	white
tehiw	April
pAirl	babies
ckgidlnu	duckweed
irsae	tadpole
ytni	duckling
ekwedcud	those
orev	tiny
sehot	over
dotlepa	raise

76 UNIT 8 Spell & Write • EMC 4539 • ©2005 by Evan-Moor Corp.

Page 77

Awesome Adjectives

Skills: Identifying Kinds of Adjectives; Identifying and Using Adjectives

Adjectives are words that describe nouns or pronouns.

- An adjective can tell what kind: old house
- An adjective can tell which one: that town
- An adjective can tell how many: two ponds

For each noun, write an adjective that tells what kind.

Responses will vary.

_______ joke _______ duckling
_______ pond _______ sweater

For each noun, write an adjective that tells which one.

_______ swan _______ fish
_______ park _______ shoes

For each noun, write an adjective that tells how many.

_______ tadpoles _______ feathers
_______ babies _______ books

©2005 by Evan-Moor Corp. • EMC 4539 • Spell & Write UNIT 8 77

Page 78

Word Study

Skills: Auditory Discrimination; Spelling Words with Long a and Long i; Spelling Theme Vocabulary; Visual Memory

Fill in the missing letters to make spelling words.

tadp o l e	th o s e	wh i t e	
duckw e e d	r a i se	d u c kling	
b a b ies	o v e r	A p ril	t i n y

Circle the words with the sound a as in bake. Underline the words with the sound i as in smile. Cross out the words with a different sound.

(babies) ~~duckling~~ ~~tadpole~~
<u>white</u> ~~those~~ ~~duckweed~~
<u>tiny</u> ~~over~~ (April) (raise)

78 UNIT 8 Spell & Write • EMC 4539 • ©2005 by Evan-Moor Corp.

Page 80

Lost Animal Baby

Skills: Writing a Creative Story

Pretend you are an animal baby that has gotten separated from its mother. You could be a duckling lost in the tall grasses, or a tadpole fleeing from a hungry swan. What happens to you? Who do you meet? How do you find your mother? Write about it below. Use as many spelling words as you can.

April white babies those over duckweed tiny duckling raise tadpole

Responses will vary.

80 UNIT 8 Spell & Write • EMC 4539 • ©2005 by Evan-Moor Corp.

Page 81

Mothers and Babies

Skills: Writing Information

Mother animals care for their babies in special ways. Mother ducks teach their babies to swim and find food. Mother frogs produce eggs and swim away. Mother swans teach their cygnets to fly. Choose one animal. Then write about how the mother cares for her babies.

Responses will vary.

Check Your Writing

- ○ I used complete sentences.
- ○ I used correct ending punctuation.
- ○ I checked my spelling.

©2005 by Evan-Moor Corp. • EMC 4539 • Spell & Write UNIT 8 81

Page 82

Test Your Skills: In the Pond

Find the correct answer. Fill in the circle.

1. Which underlined word is an adjective?
   - ● <u>Tiny</u> tadpoles fill the pond.
   - ○ We took <u>pictures</u> of the ducklings.
   - ○ The ducklings <u>look</u> lost.
2. Which underlined word is an adjective?
   - ○ The <u>tadpoles</u> disappeared.
   - ● The <u>white</u> swan swam fast.
   - ○ The ducklings <u>learned</u> how to swim.
3. Which word is spelled correctly?
   - ○ rayse
   - ○ raize
   - ● raise
4. Which word means "very small"?
   - ● tiny
   - ○ tadpole
   - ○ babies

My Spelling Test

Ask someone to test you on the spelling words.

1. ________
2. ________
3. ________
4. ________
5. ________
6. ________
7. ________
8. ________
9. ________
10. ________

5. Write the sentence correctly.

can thoz wite duck babys find the pond

Can those white duck babies find the pond?

82 ASSESSMENT 8 Spell & Write • EMC 4539 • ©2005 by Evan-Moor Corp.

Page 83

Zoo Quiz

Is your favorite animal at the zoo
Smarter than an elephant?
Smarter than you?
More useful than a monkey
Or a chimpanzee or two?
More fearless than a lion?
More careless than a kangaroo?
Which one is the happiest?
The snake? The bear? The gnu?
Which one is the funniest?
Or fastest at the zoo?
I think I like the tiger.
Do you have a favorite, too?
Tell me, yes, please do!

Find It! Read the spelling words. Check off the words you can find in the story.

✓ useful ✓ smarter ✓ fastest ✓ funniest ✓ happiest
✓ fearless ✓ careless ☐ feed ☐ clean ✓ animal

How many spelling words did you find? 8

Page 85

Find the Words

Write the missing words to complete the sentences.

1. Do you think cheetahs are fastest or happiest?
   animal fastest happiest feed
2. Zookeepers feed and clean the animals.
   fearless useful feed clean
3. The lion is said to be a fearless animal.
   animal funniest fearless fastest
4. I think elephants are smarter than zebras.
   useful clean smarter careless
5. Many animals are useful to humans.
   happiest smarter feed useful
6. Monkeys are the funniest animals in the zoo!
   feed clean funniest animal

Page 86

What Does It Mean?

Look at the meanings of the suffixes in the box. Then write the spelling word for each definition.

less = without ful = full of er = more est = most

useful smarter fastest funniest happiest
fearless careless feed clean animal

1. more intelligent smarter
2. most happy happiest
3. without care careless
4. most fast fastest
5. full of use useful
6. without fear fearless
7. most funny funniest

Page 87

Comparing Words

An adjective tells about a noun. An adjective can make comparisons.

- Use er to compare two people, places, or things.
  Elephants are taller than zebras.
- Use est to compare three or more people, places, or things.
  Giraffes are the tallest animals in the zoo.

Write the correct adjective in the blank.

1. The zookeeper is the smartest person in the zoo. (smarter / smartest)
2. The green snakes are longer than the striped snakes. (longer / longest)
3. The toucan has brighter feathers than the flamingo. (brighter / brightest)
4. Simba the lion is the largest in his pride. (larger / largest)
5. That is the loudest roar I've ever heard! (louder / loudest)
6. Champ the chimp is the oldest monkey here. (older / oldest)

Page 88

Make a Match

Write the letter of the definition next to the word.

e	1. useful	a. not paying close attention
h	2. fearless	b. to give food to
i	3. smarter	c. causing the most laughter
a	4. careless	d. free from dirt
j	5. fastest	e. helpful
b	6. feed	f. a living thing that is not a plant
c	7. funniest	g. most cheerful
d	8. clean	h. unafraid
g	9. happiest	i. more intelligent or clever
f	10. animal	j. moving the quickest

Page 90

Zoo Questions

Use words from "Zoo Quiz" to answer these questions about zoo animals.

1. Which zoo animal do you think is smart?
   Responses will vary.
2. Which zoo animal do you think is fearless?
3. Which zoo animal do you think is fast?
4. Which zoo animal do you think is funny?
5. Which zoo animal do you think is useful?

Page 91

Backyard Zoo

The zookeeper said you could bring home three animals from the zoo! Which animals would you choose? Describe how you would keep and care for them. Use some of the spelling words.

useful smarter fastest funniest happiest
fearless careless feed clean animal

Responses will vary.

Check Your Writing
- ☐ I used complete sentences.
- ☐ I used commas correctly.
- ☐ I checked my spelling.

Page 92

Test Your Skills: Zoo Quiz

Find the correct answer. Fill in the circle.

1. Which adjective correctly completes this sentence?
   Jenny's cat is ____ than her dog.
   - ○ fluffy
   - ● fluffier
   - ○ fluffiest
2. Which adjective correctly completes this sentence?
   Which giraffe's neck is the ____ in the group?
   - ○ long
   - ○ longer
   - ● longest
3. Which word is spelled correctly?
   - ○ happyest
   - ○ happiess
   - ● happiest
4. Which word means "free from dirt"?
   - ● clean
   - ○ feed
   - ○ useful

My Spelling Test

Ask someone to test you on the spelling words.

1. ____ 2. ____ 3. ____ 4. ____ 5. ____ 6. ____ 7. ____ 8. ____ 9. ____ 10. ____

5. Write the sentence correctly.
   i think the feerliss lion is a smarttr animul than the zebra
   I think the fearless lion is a smarter animal than the zebra.

Page 93

Breakfast Is Served

On Saturday morning, my older brother Chris and I got up early. We wanted to make a surprise breakfast for our mother. I helped measure the milk, and then Chris showed me how to break the eggs. We cut up some bread cubes and put them in a baking dish. We poured the milk and eggs over the bread, and I sprinkled on some cheese. Then it was time for baking. I put it in the oven for twenty minutes. When Mom heard the timer go off, she came into the kitchen. Was she surprised to find a delicious breakfast ready to eat!

Find It! Read the spelling words. Check off the words you can find in the story.

✓ early ✓ heard ___ friend ✓ eat ✓ measure
✓ break ✓ brother ✓ mother ✓ bread ✓ oven

How many spelling words did you find? 9

©2005 by Evan-Moor Corp. • EMC 4539 • Spell & Write UNIT 10 93

Page 95

Spell It

Skills: Spelling Words with ea; Spelling Theme Vocabulary; Visual Memory

Circle the word in each row that is spelled correctly.

1.	hurd	(heard)	herde
2.	owen	ovun	(oven)
3.	muther	(mother)	mothre
4.	(friend)	frend	freind
5.	(eat)	eet	eate
6.	erly	urley	(early)
7.	mesurre	(measure)	meassur
8.	(brother)	bruther	broethr
9.	brak	breek	(break)
10.	(bread)	brede	breadd

©2005 by Evan-Moor Corp. • EMC 4539 • Spell & Write UNIT 10 95

Page 96

Crossword Challenge

Skills: Spelling Words with ea; Spelling Theme Vocabulary; Matching Words with Their Meanings

Complete the crossword puzzle using the spelling words.

early heard friend eat measure
break brother mother bread oven

Down
1. a boy or man who has the same parents as another person
2. to have sensed sounds through your ears
4. a baked food made from flour, water, and often yeast
5. an enclosed space where food is baked or roasted
6. a female parent
7. before the usual time

Across
3. someone whom you know well and enjoy being with
6. to find out the size, capacity, or weight of something
8. to take in food through the mouth
9. to damage something so that it is in pieces

96 UNIT 10 Spell & Write • EMC 4539 • ©2005 by Evan-Moor Corp.

Page 97

Action and Helping Verbs

Skills: Identifying and Using Action and Helping Verbs

A verb tells what is happening to the noun.
• Action verbs show an action.
measure, cook, break, eat
• Helping verbs come before the main verb to tell about the action.
will, has, had, have, could, would, should, do, does, did

Write the correct verb in the blank. Then write A for action or H for helping in the box after the sentence.

1. In the morning, I feel the warm sun on my face. (sleep / would / feel) A
2. Let's make breakfast for Mother. (make / should / am) A
3. I know he will snooze and snore. (was / have / will) H
4. Eggs and bacon sizzle in the pan. (sizzle / am / will) A
5. We could make tasty pancakes, too. (does / could / is) H

©2005 by Evan-Moor Corp. • EMC 4539 • Spell & Write UNIT 10 97

Page 98

Word Study

Skills: Auditory Discrimination; Visual Memory

Say each word aloud. Then write it next to the correct sound.

heard measure eat bread break early

1. a as in bake: break
2. e as in bed: bread, measure
3. ir as in bird: heard, early
4. e as in weak: eat

Fill in the missing letters.

1. br o th e r
2. fr i e nd
3. m o th e r
4. o v e n

98 UNIT 10 Spell & Write • EMC 4539 • ©2005 by Evan-Moor Corp.

Page 100

My Favorite Recipe

Skills: Writing a Recipe

What is a favorite food that you can make yourself? Write your favorite recipe below. Remember to write the steps in order.

Recipe for: ______

You will need: Responses will vary.

1. ______
2. ______
3. ______
4. ______
5. ______
6. ______

100 UNIT 10 Spell & Write • EMC 4539 • ©2005 by Evan-Moor Corp.

Page 101

Special Gift

Skills: Writing a Personal Narrative

The children in the story are making a special breakfast for their mother. What special gifts have you received? Write about a time when someone gave you a wonderful gift.

Responses will vary.

Check Your Writing
- I wrote complete sentences.
- I used correct punctuation.
- I checked my spelling.

©2005 by Evan-Moor Corp. • EMC 4539 • Spell & Write UNIT 10 101

Page 102

Test Your Skills: Breakfast Is Served

Find the correct answer. Fill in the circle.

1. In which sentence is the underlined word an action verb?
   - Shania is an excellent cook.
   - Shania has big dreams.
   - ● Shania bakes delicious pies.
2. In which sentence is the helping verb underlined?
   - ● Trey will make dinner tonight.
   - He likes steak and baked potatoes.
   - We brought the dessert.
3. Which word is spelled correctly?
   - meazhur
   - ● measure
   - meshure
4. Which word means "an enclosed space where food is baked"?
   - ● oven
   - eat
   - bread

My Spelling Test

Ask someone to test you on the spelling words.

1. ______
2. ______
3. ______
4. ______
5. ______
6. ______
7. ______
8. ______
9. ______
10. ______

5. Write the sentence correctly.
muthr's frends is coming eurly to bake bredd
Mother's friends are coming early to bake bread.

102 ASSESSMENT 10 Spell & Write • EMC 4539 • ©2005 by Evan-Moor Corp.

Page 103

Once upon a Time

Long, long ago, Princess Dahlia sat in her room in the castle. On this dreamy night, Dahlia thought about her future. She wished to be a squire, just like her brother. Then someday, she could become a knight! Dahlia loved each story about the knights' bravery as they brought peace to the land. Their skills in war were unmatched. Their adventures seemed endless. Dahlia longed to have her own adventures out there in the world. She closed her eyes to think what her life might be like. Suddenly, she felt something enter her room. When Dahlia opened her eyes, the room was full of golden light.

She was dressed in a suit of shining armor! A shield was ready at her side. She was about to begin a new adventure!

Find It! Read the spelling words. Check off the words you can find in the story.

✓ war ✓ night ✓ knight ☐ piece ✓ peace
✓ their ✓ there ✓ castle ✓ story ✓ princess

How many spelling words did you find? 9

 UNIT 11 103

Page 105

Sound Search

Skills: Homophones; Spelling Theme Vocabulary; Synonyms and Antonyms

Say the words in the box aloud. Write the two words that sound the same on the lines.

night peace there wore
piece their war knight

1.	night knight	3.	their there
2.	piece peace	4.	war wore

What spelling word means the opposite of ____?

war peace
here there
day night

What spelling word means the same as ____?

part piece
tale story
belonging to them their

 UNIT 11 105

Page 106

Super Spellings

Skills: Homophones; Spelling Theme Vocabulary; Visual Memory

Circle the word that correctly completes each sentence.

1. It was a dark, starry knight/(night)
2. The (knight)/night wore a suit of shining armor.
3. They spread (peace)/piece across the land.
4. A peace/(piece) of her dream came true.
5. She saw the shield their/(there) in the corner.
6. The knights gave (their)/there all to the war.

Circle the words that are spelled correctly.

peece	(story)	prinsces	cassle
(castle)	nitek	(night)	(peace)
wor	ther	(war)	(princess)
(their)	peice	(there)	(night)

106 UNIT 11

Page 107

Correcting Capitals

Skills: Using Capital Letters; Writing Complete Sentences

Correct the words that need capital letters. Cross out the small letter and write the capital letter above it.

July	morning	Dr. Barns
Labor Day	Thursday	week
Mr. Gonzales	sister	Brett
teacher	Ms. Spencer	Halloween

Circle the letters that should be capitalized. Then rewrite the sentences.

1. at night, the princess dreamed of king william.
At night, the princess dreamed of King William.
2. is saturday dahlia's favorite day of the week?
Is Saturday Dahlia's favorite day of the week?
3. "i practice sword fighting on tuesdays," the knight said.
"I practice sword fighting on Tuesdays," the knight said.
4. the gallant prince john rode the white steed.
The gallant Prince John rode the white steed.
5. "would you like to be a squire?" the fairy asked.
"Would you like to be a squire?" the fairy asked.

 UNIT 11 107

Page 108

Word Search

Skills: Visual Sequencing; Recognizing Spelling Words

Find and circle the spelling words. Words can go across, down, or diagonally.

war night knight piece peace
their there castle story princess

T	E	N	D	E	R	H	A	R	T	O	T
T	O	P	I	E	C	E	Z	H	A	N	D
H	H	E	R	U	G	S	G	O	T	D	N
E	O	G	H	I	P	I	N	O	L	D	A
I	B	S	I	S	N	O	R	A	Y	O	L
R	O	S	E	N	O	C	W	A	R	E	G
P	E	A	C	E	K	O	E	X	O	L	N
I	A	T	A	N	K	C	A	S	T	L	E
E	R	E	H	T	H	E	N	O	S	E	S

108 UNIT 11

Page 110

What Happened Next?

Skills: Writing a Fairy Tale

What do you think happened to Dahlia after she got her suit of armor and her shield? Write about her new adventures. Use as many spelling words as you can.

war night knight piece peace
their there castle story princess

Responses will vary.

Check Your Writing

- ○ I used capital letters correctly.
- ○ I wrote complete sentences.
- ○ I checked my spelling.

110 UNIT 11

Page 111

The Perfect Knight

Skills: Writing a List

Knights in the Middle Ages lived by a strict code. This code included rules about honor and bravery. What do you think are important skills for a knight to have? Strong? Polite? Brave? List eight skills below.

1. Responses will vary.
2.
3.
4.
5.
6.
7.
8.

 UNIT 11 111

Page 112

Test Your Skills: Once upon a Time

Find the correct answer. Fill in the circle.

1. Which sentence has correct capital letters?
   - ○ king george knighted james on Sunday.
   - ○ King george Knighted James on sunday.
   - ● King George knighted James on Sunday.
2. Which sentence has correct capital letters?
   - ○ dahlia wanted to be a knight for halloween.
   - ○ Dahlia wanted to be a knight for halloween.
   - ● Dahlia wanted to be a knight for Halloween.
3. Which word is spelled correctly?
   - ● castle
   - ○ cassle
   - ○ cassel
4. Which word means "the time between sunset and sunrise"?
   - ○ story
   - ○ war
   - ● night

My Spelling Test

Ask someone to test you on the spelling words.

1. ____
2. ____
3. ____
4. ____
5. ____
6. ____
7. ____
8. ____
9. ____
10. ____

5. Write the sentence correctly.
the knite's storey of peese spread through the land
The knight's story of peace spread through the land.

112 ASSESSMENT 11

Page 113

Postcard from Mexico

Dear Jordan,
Here is your postcard from Mexico. We are having a really fun vacation. The beach here is beautiful, and the sand is white like sugar. The air is so warm that we can wear our summer clothes, even at night! The people are friendly, too.
Yesterday we rented a sailboat. You should have seen the color of the ocean. It was bright blue, and we could see all the way to the bottom! The water was as warm as a bath. Every day, we eat all of our favorite Mexican foods. This is a vacation to remember. Wish you were here!
Your friend,
Ana

Find It! Read the spelling words. Check off the words you can find in the story.

✓ air ✓ beautiful ✓ vacation ✓ sailboat ✓ people
✓ favorite ✓ remember ☐ suitcase ✓ postcard ✓ clothes

How many spelling words did you find? 9

©2005 by Evan-Moor Corp. • EMC 4539 • Spell & Write UNIT 12 113

Page 115

Circle and Spell

Skills: Compound Words; Spelling Theme Vocabulary; Visual Memory

Circle the word in each row that is spelled correctly.

1.	(clothes)	clothz	cloese
2.	sutecas	(suitcase)	sootcase
3.	butiful	(beautiful)	beutifull
4.	peeple	pepole	(people)
5.	(air)	aer	aire
6.	postkerd	posttcarde	(postcard)
7.	faverit	(favorite)	faverote
8.	(remember)	remmembr	rememmber
9.	salebote	saillboate	(sailboat)
10.	(vacation)	vakashion	vacasion

©2005 by Evan-Moor Corp. • EMC 4539 • Spell & Write UNIT 12 115

Page 116

Building Words

Skills: Compound Words; Spelling Theme Vocabulary; Visual Memory

Fill in the missing letters to make spelling words.

1.	b e a utif u l	6.	s u i tc a se
2.	cl o t h es	7.	p e o pl e
3.	a i r	8.	rem e m b e r
4.	fav o r i te	9.	postc a r d
5.	s a i lbo a t	10.	vaca t i o n

Draw a line between the words to make compound spelling words. Write the words on the lines.

sail — boat: sailboat
suit — case: suitcase
post — card: postcard

116 UNIT 12 Spell & Write • EMC 4539 • ©2005 by Evan-Moor Corp.

Page 117

Word Search

Skills: Visual Sequencing; Recognizing Spelling Words

Find and circle the spelling words. Words can go across, down, or diagonally.

air, beautiful, favorite, clothes, people, vacation, remember, suitcase, postcard, sailboat

W	T	E	P	O	S	T	C	A	R	D	C
S	A	I	L	B	O	A	T	L	S	P	S
R	C	P	S	T	Q	E	U	H	Y	E	V
E	A	E	L	U	A	F	R	Y	H	I	A
F	A	V	O	R	I	T	E	T	D	E	C
R	U	I	A	T	R	T	O	I	L	R	A
I	E	W	U	H	Y	L	C	P	J	S	T
S	L	A	C	N	C	R	O	A	E	P	I
R	E	M	E	M	B	E	R	T	S	O	O
B	R	O	A	T	P	R	U	B	S	E	N

©2005 by Evan-Moor Corp. • EMC 4539 • Spell & Write UNIT 12 117

Page 118

When Did It Happen?

Skills: Identifying and Using Past, Present, and Future Verb Tenses; Writing Complete Sentences

A verb can show action. The tense of a verb tells when an action occurs.
- present—the action is happening now. We are swimming.
- past—the action already happened. I swam yesterday.
- future—the action is going to happen. Tomorrow I will swim.

Rewrite this sentence in the present tense and then the past tense.
Tanya will write a postcard to her friend.
1. Tanya is writing a postcard to her friend.
2. Tanya wrote a postcard to her friend.

Rewrite this sentence in the past tense and then the future tense.
Marco feels the warm sand between his toes.
1. Marco felt the warm sand between his toes.
2. Marco will feel the warm sand between his toes.

Rewrite this sentence in the present and then the future tense.
Jake and Kaitlin sailed on their vacation.
1. Jake and Kaitlin are sailing on their vacation.
2. Jake and Kaitlin will sail on their vacation.

118 UNIT 12 Spell & Write • EMC 4539 • ©2005 by Evan-Moor Corp.

Page 120

Postcard to a Friend

Skills: Writing a Postcard

What kinds of trips have you taken? Have you visited a museum, the zoo, or the beach? Write a postcard to a friend telling about your trip. Use as many spelling words as you can.

air, beautiful, favorite, clothes, people, vacation, remember, suitcase, postcard, sailboat

Responses will vary.

To:

Check Your Writing
- I used a capital letter to begin each sentence.
- I wrote complete sentences.
- I checked my spelling.

120 UNIT 12 Spell & Write • EMC 4539 • ©2005 by Evan-Moor Corp.

Page 121

My Favorite Places

Skills: Writing Descriptions

On the postcard, Ana describes Mexico to her friend. Think of three of your favorite places. Describe what you like about each place.

Favorite Place #1:
Responses will vary.

Favorite Place #2:

Favorite Place #3:

©2005 by Evan-Moor Corp. • EMC 4539 • Spell & Write UNIT 12 121

Page 122

Test Your Skills: Postcard from Mexico

Find the correct answer. Fill in the circle.

1. Which tense is the verb in this sentence?
Jordan will read his postcard after school.
○ past
○ present
● future

2. Which tense is the verb in this sentence?
Ana travels to Mexico every summer.
○ past
● present
○ future

3. Which word is spelled correctly?
● sailboat
○ sailbote
○ saillboate

4. Which word means "the mixture of gases that surround the Earth"?
○ people
● air
○ beautiful

5. Write the sentence correctly.
remumbr to bring your favurit clothz
Remember to bring your favorite clothes.

My Spelling Test

Ask someone to test you on the spelling words.

1.
2.
3.
4.
5.
6.
7.
8.
9.
10.

122 ASSESSMENT 12 Spell & Write • EMC 4539 • ©2005 by Evan-Moor Corp.